D0605087

Still Waters

Prepared in conjunction
with the *Nova* film *Still
Waters*, produced by Peace
River Films for WGBH
Educational Foundation

By Alexandra Marshall
Still Waters
Gus in Bronze

Still Waters

by Alexandra Marshall

William Morrow and Company, Inc. · New York · 1978

Library of Congress Cataloging in Publication Data

Marshall, Alexandra.
  Still waters.

  1. Pond ecology. I. WGBH Educational Foundation.
II. Title.
QH541.5.P63M34   574.5′2632   78-18723
ISBN 0-688-03342-3

Printed in the United States of America.

First Edition
1 2 3 4 5 6 7 8 9 10

Foreword

In spite of the fact that there are over two million ponds in this country, there existed no film of any length about the ecology of a North American freshwater pond. This was the impulse behind the idea for *Still Waters,* and it originated with WGBH, the Boston Public Television station. Peace River Films, a Cambridge company whose principals are Neil Goodwin and John Borden, and who had made two other films for WGBH Boston's *Nova,* was then commissioned to develop a proposal for such a film. They responded with a treatment that shaped the idea into a year-long study of a Massachusetts beaver pond.

This book was seen as a parallel observation of the same pond over the same period of time. It was arranged that Neil and John would double as film makers and still photographers, securing in addition to their own pictures those of two other naturalist photographers, Jack Swedberg and Peter Schweitzer, and that I would write the book around which to arrange their pictures.

Often the technological advantages of photography provided solutions for me as well as for Neil and John. The problem in observing nature at close hand is always how to see what one needs to see and not disrupt it, and their ingenuity made it possible that they, and consequently that I too, had a shot at what is impossible to see without technological intervention. I quickly learned from them the fundamental technique of observation: one goes into the field, sets up, sits, and waits. If and when something happens, one simply tries to be there for it.

Two other people at Peace River Films greatly facilitated the project with input and outlay. Margot Barnes catalogued and cross-indexed photographs, and Lee Nameche gathered and sorted research on every aspect of pond life. Lee interpreted data for me, and she initiated me into and guided me through the sophisticated world I hoped to render accessible to others.

There have been many questions and many answers. If Peace River Films and I viewed the pond from the same place initially, we brought to it differing expertise and interests and soon began seeing the pond from separate angles. The diversity of our ways of observing enriched the project, but the text of this book reflects only my own experience of those questions and answers.

I am grateful to my husband, James Carroll, who believes as I do in biting off almost more than can be chewed, and who was with me.

ALEXANDRA MARSHALL
Boston, Massachusetts
January, 1978

Table of Contents

Color Plates

2

3

5

6

7

8

10

11

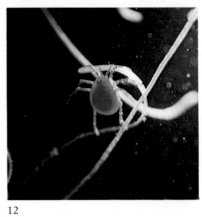

12

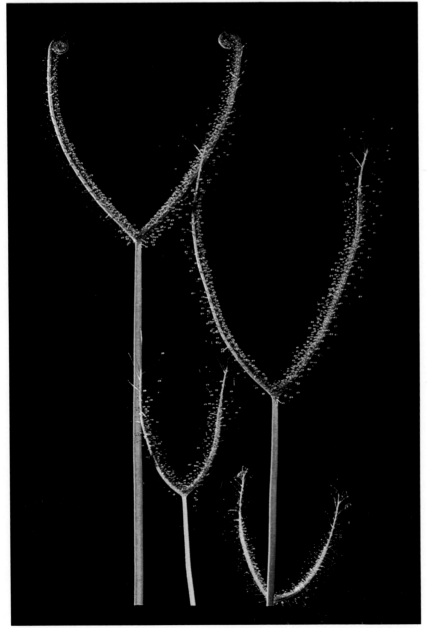

13

14

15

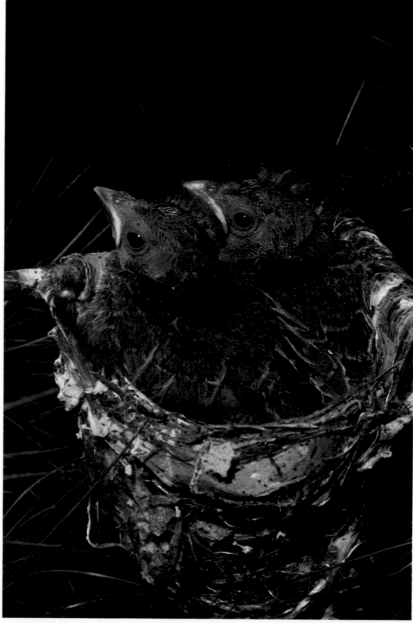

16

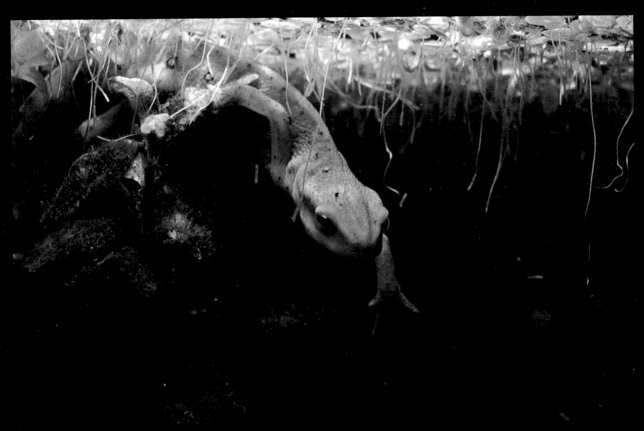

17

20

18

19

22

21

24

25

26

29

30

31

32

Temper Brook

This is my first season at the pond I am going to keep under surveillance for a year, and it is a dim winter morning in January chosen for flying over it. Four of us, the pilot and I and two photographers at work on the *Still Waters* film and the pictures for this book, have taken off in a plane not much bigger than a Cadillac, powered by a prop that whisks the air as if it were egg white. The rural Massachusetts countryside underneath us is just that: villages, clusters of farm buildings, fields, forest, all of which from higher up would make a pointillist landscape blended by the eye but which instead, from just above, makes a primitive. An off-kilter horse stands under the eve of a barn that isn't quite three-dimensional; stubs of corn stalks are uncovered by snow wind-blown elsewhere and look like whiskers coming in. Walls and fences lose function, since who would want to trespass anyway? Smoke puffs up from chimneys, but it looks tentative and dissipates quickly. The monochrome is a chilly stillness.

The nearing evergreen forest is an Army blanket suddenly, and the ponds are ragged-edged holes in it. Acres of frozen water have been created by beavers who first dammed the Temper Brook twenty years ago and who have since developed the area to village proportions. Lodges mound up like scoops of vanilla ice cream topped with molasses sauce, in fact mud where the cover of snow has melted around the vent which allows air in and gases out. Dams cinch the pond in various places, on the pulses that would be barely audible now, in winter, but that will throb with the thaw. We are flying one hundred feet off the ground at a speed, which is why I think Cadillac, of only sixty-five miles an hour.

We bank and circle to keep a view of the deer who are well camouflaged against the patchy snow covering. They huddle in their herd, foraging, ferreting out the meager winter offerings, pawing, nosing, nudging one another. I keep them in the binocular's eye as we spiral hawkishly.

Tracks trail across the snowed-over ice and mass around each perforation in the pond's winter skin, where the water runs too fast to freeze or where beavers have purposely guarded an

oxygen access they need only supplementally, given that they winter in their vented lodges. The tracks are in predatory concentration around their lodges, but they are futile. The lodges are utterly impregnable fortresses in which the beaver, relatively stuporous but not dormant, waits for the birth of the kits after the early-winter mating.

Two crows shuffle where the snow is crustless and step their way across the bare parts. They are doubtless not the only birds out looking for eats, but I see only them, their black on the white a plausible target to fix with the glass as we fly overhead. As the crow flies, as the saying goes, the distance from the bottommost dam to the top of the head pond is somewhat less than a mile. Were we counting the contours it would be many more than one, since the ponds bulge and taper to shape the system into resembling the finely interlocking chain that is DNA.

Which is apt enough. What the beaver has done with the forested land, in preventing it from maturing to its otherwise rather uniform state, is to create instead an ecosystem that is benign to a large range of other creatures because it is abundantly rich in life supports. In damming the Temper Brook, beavers have stilled it and flooded the forest floor to a depth of five or six feet. The stilled water fills with life-forms that are part of the complex, faithful relationship out of which each depends on the other for food and shelter and reproduction. And all of this is realized as a by-product of the beaver's own agenda. What the beaver does, alone with man among mammals, is habitually, radically to alter its environment to suit the needs of its life-style. What audacity, what common sense.

Originally the land was forested, then cleared for cultivation, then abandoned and returned to forest, then recultivated by the beaver. From the air, especially in winter's minimal landscape, the area seems to be a double exposure. One sees, as if a superimposition, fields of evergreen trees neatly bounded by ancient stone walls. The plant ecologist's term for this is succession, which means simply the return from forest to forest.

5   Temper Brook

The land-clearing peak in New England occurred around 1830, but land around the Temper Brook remained cultivated for another hundred years before it was abandoned. Cellar holes and the odd junked chassis attest to homesteads, even to the little village that used to be there, called Mill Village. The old roads, preserved by conservationists, meander through the remains of the evacuated settlement, squaring off at the stone corners to make crossroads that now only animals travel. The fields have grown up evergreen, but the walls are still there. And what was once Mill Village now is farmed by beavers.

The flooding gives access by water to the trees beavers need for food or building, and the trees are cut from the woods that border the pond and from the pond itself. The swamped trees not taken go prematurely orange and then bare, drowning, rotting, collapsing to the bottom to decay away. The stumps that remain stick up like thumbs, and even they, and even in winter, appear to grow, when in fact they are among the obvious casualties of an ecosystem that trades in countless deaths for the bonus of births by the billions.

The ice is a platform. Under it lie unused the stage-prop objects whose purpose comes clear only during a performance. Overwintering eggs wait under the ice, or are sealed in it, for the season and the play in which they feature. Reptiles and amphibians are dug into the pond's muddy bottom, body temperature dropped to the just above zero that keeps them alive but otherwise utterly functionless. Fish hang like costumes on hangers, and plants lie about like hats in need of accessorizing. As if all of winter were a Monday, this theatre under the ice is dark.

On top, a living is scavenged by any who haven't the habit of hibernating, or who haven't managed an adequate food supply. A deer carcass, dropped for the kill probably after a chase by dogs, lies on the ice like a banquet table. The predators have feasted, with the leftovers going to any nonvegetarian scavenger who can get near enough. There are eagles no doubt, invisible because scared off by the plane engine, hanging

around to finish their picking. I've seen them other days ripping at the tattered hides of other dead deer, using their talons for leverage and their beaks for prying the flesh off the bones.

More reliable are the branches stockpiled by beavers in an underwater food cache near the entrance to their lodges, a winter food supply which will be supplemented by excess body fat accumulated with easy living in easier seasons. Creatures that cache, like the squirrel and the bluejay, hide nuts where they can and, if the supply is adequately gauged, survive to feed again in earnest. It can be an unsympathetic landscape for those who don't plan ahead, or accurately.

We go up to turn and come down again for a last slow pass, and I am invited to take the controls. Hawks glide on currents for whole migrations, and so do butterflies, placing themselves like luggage on conveyor belts of air. I wish I could have that feeling. I'm told this plane is impossible to stall, and yet I'm hard to convince that I won't inadvertently tip up the nose and drop us like a death-wishing hang glider. It took me years to discover that birds stop by stalling and by cushioning airflow with outstretched wings, and not by coming in on their bellies. In all my childhood flying dreams I had ladder legs, folding yardstick legs to keep me from chin-first landings that would wreck my wings. I never knew how it worked, only that it somehow did, and by the time I figured it out about flight I'd moved on to deep-sea dolphin dreams and mermaid fantasies.

Birds stop by stalling. The televised first landing of the Concorde struck me because it resembled nothing fancier than a tree swallow planing in beak first, tipping up, sinking somewhat, and touching down at the entrance to its nest in the stump of a root-swamped tree bereft of bark and branches. I've seen eagles play by falling down chutes of air in canyons: they tip and drop sideways, they freefall, they scoop themselves up before crashing. A hummingbird stalls to drink and has to vibrate its wings almost faster than the speed of sight in order not to drop like a pebble. Lucky us who stop by stopping.

I give back the controls with relief and suggest still one more final pass for thinking, not of our stall (I don't believe it's impossible), but of the stall the pond is below us. I think of glass being blown by an expert: molten, it flows controlled through rounded shape after shape until it is fixed, cooled. It's as if the pond too were blown from that point along the brook where it begins, and blown again at each bulge, and blown wide and narrow, shallow and deep all the way down to the foot. Imagine the pond a vessel, a vase whose color is only what it reflects: spring lemon-lime, summer emerald, autumn toast, and winter.

Winter what? Winter ghost, I think it is, winter disembodied hauntings, dim and dull but not substanceless. Winter rest for revitalization, but also winter glum, low clouds, deprivation, edginess, heavy-mooded wintery owl-hooting hollowness. Echoes. The stall: the time between activities, itself empty.

This time I barely see even tracks, I see so little evidence reflected from what lives there. There isn't, granted, much that does, or that will show itself in winter, but still: there were deer and crows and fresh tracks, and the snow was melting on the beaver lodge as an indicator of heat being generated within. There were the pointy evergreens, the skeletal birches, the scaffoldlike other hardwoods. There was the carcass. But none of it shows up, not to mention giving up its color to the cloudy vessel of motion stalled, poised in suspension, on the near edge of emptiness.

Up again and making for the rural runway, the landscape is full once more. Kids are playing hockey on a farm pond, steeples peak up cheerily, asphalt bands a town up and connects to the next and next. There are stone walls that once bordered fields and still do, the forest having been held off in favor of row or forage crops. All is tidiness, Mom-and-Dad land, the always-have-been or back-to-the-soil life. Winter here seems an afternoon nap, instead of the coma it is at the pond.

And yet it is finally exactly because of the extremes that the pond is interesting beyond measure. Just as winter's zero numbs with isolation, so will spring be the grandest chaos. On a farm there's as little waste as possible: goats and tomatoes are numbered in proportion to the family's size, and hence the orderliness of daily life. At the pond the ratios are raggedier. The numbers for some species are literally incalculable, beyond billions into the zillions that are silly with zeros and commas. The proportions are only approximate, and all is based, generation after generation, on trial and error.

The beaver colony couldn't be as big were it in civilization. Cage traps would be set, and some would be relocated onto some part of the land that wasn't somebody's. Roads get flooded and woods get mulched and crops get drenched and grazing land gets inundated; and farmers get mad, and no wonder. And then beaver pairs get split up—they otherwise mate for life—and then kits have no adults to learn from, and so what's it all for anyway? Better by far when the beavers keep themselves out of the way, as they've managed at Temper Brook, where the zoning is in their favor.

But it's ironic. Beavers are responsible for some of the most fertile land in the country. When they move on from a pond and the dam collapses to spill the water out, what is left is the richest soil going, valleys that can be as lush with land life as once they were with water. We have, at least, a relationship of mutualism with beavers. And much more, some say.

Beavers have been revered by North American Indians for centuries, but as far as I know, only the Cherokee creation mythology features them as stars. According to Cherokee legend, the Great Spirit deputized beavers and awarded them the responsibility for creation by instructing them to dive to the bottom of the sea for soil out of which to build the earth's landmasses. Which they did.

You can't imagine it? Listen to this: a million years ago in the Pleistocene era, beaver ancestors, the Castoroides, were giants

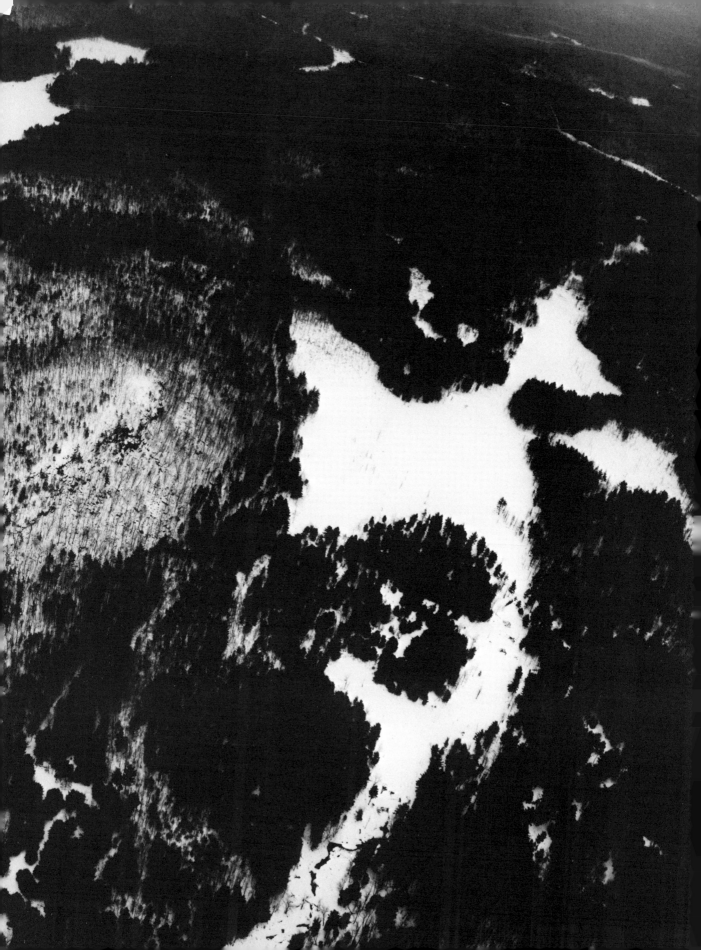

who weighed seven hundred pounds and had skills, apparently, from which those of the present-day beaver have been derived.

The Temper Brook pond is nothing. There's a beaver dam in New Hampshire that's reported to stretch for four thousand feet to create a lake around which forty lodges are built. Their dams and their lodges are constructed with pond bottom, stones, logs, and branches piled up to make islands, peninsulas, continents.

I can imagine that beavers created the earth the way the Cherokee have it. As a theory it even beats, in my opinion, almost, science.

Human beings need the down and fur of other animals in order to survive winter's cold, and our dwellings must have insulation and heated air. We tend to think therefore that winter is cruel to all species; it isn't, in fact.

Other species adapt in several ways: with migration capabilities, with increases in body fat and the development of winter coats, and with the ability to remain dormant. Many animals and plants make of winter a time to rest, suspending animation for the long duration.

The winter hideouts at the pond can be the undersides of leaves, can be crevices, tunnels, or dens in banks, can be between the bark and the tree, can be dugouts in the mud on the bottom, or air spaces in the stems of plants, or lodges built expressly, or lodges abandoned and taken by squatters, or pecked holes in standing wood (or gnawed in fallen), can be under rocks and in stone walls and can even be in the ice itself.

There is no way to know how many there are hidden away, but let me share some figures given by Franklin Russell in his *Watchers at the Pond* and let us know only that at Temper Brook there are more or fewer. Ladybugs numbering 120,000 burrow deep into their hibernaculum; the earthworm hibernates in knots of sixty to a thousand, and Russell estimates that around his pond are dormant earthworms to the tune of five hundred million. Several thousand ants survive encasement in ice when rainwater seeps into their crevice and freezes. Count in cells and you have inertia on the billion scale, on the multibillion scale.

And then there's the bumblebee queen who, like the wasp queen, winters as the sole survivor of the hive and lives to give birth to the year's population. The queen is the sleeping potential of the race and counts for momentous numbers, the way an unstruck match counts for hundreds of thousands of acres of flammable forest land.

The way China's population, when we first heard the figures and still for some now, is unthinkable, so is it a staggering conception that at the pond there can be so many *bodies* that for

the most part come equipped with eyes and limbs and some kind of nervous system. Better let me amend that: in truth it is far more thinkable that there are a billion just like us in China than that dug in the banks of a medium-sized pond there are a half-billion earthworms.

But hence the "appeal" of the horror films in which all that is horrible is that there are far too many of whatever: birds, locusts, bats, rats, bugs, snakes, you name it. I once was made nauseous by ants. I opened the envelope of aluminum foil in which I was keeping a piece of cake, and dozens of glossy black ants danced out. Granted, that kind of surprise will always be unnerving, and nobody wants to discover there are ants in the food; still, what was too much for my stomach was that too many were grouped in too small a place. In their scramble for escape their legs clanged against the foil and sounded as if each ant were wearing three pairs of tap shoes for clattering out the frenzied message that was their alarm. Far too many legs. Far too many sleepers at the pond, far too many eggs of all varieties, far too many zeros on the ends of their numbers.

And yet: to stay alive, just to keep on hanging in there as a nonextinct species, a generation has to do more than reproduce itself once and a half. The casualties are unspeakably heavy by human standards, which both goes without saying and must be said. A chickadee, for instance, pecks at tree bark on a winter day and eats five hundred aphid eggs. A mole breaks into an earthworm hibernaculum and downs a few hundred of them. Adults who cannot survive a winter leave thousands of eggs behind to keep even with the odds that most won't make it. And every species is sized, for the most part, large or small in correct proportion to its environment. Tally up all the zeros and they cancel each other.

Trial and error is what we go by as children before our powers to reason are fully developed, before we know what estimates are. Nature always goes by trial and error. It balances as a watchmaker does the minutest gears of a pocket watch, as an accountant does the books in black and red. Nature is accountable for winter in the creatures that multiply practically to infinity. It recompenses for dirty tricks and compensates for slipups. Nature is the only agency that insures its clients even against an act of God.

A day at the pond in winter is a short one telescoped by the long dark on either side of it. Dawn heads up a pale dusty-rose, turns to yellow, then a thin orange, thinner gold, again yellow, and then loses itself through diffusion into gray and behind low-slung clouds. And gray the sky stays, like the felt hat of an Englishman, as if hung on a peg for the working day.

Grass tussocks from which needles of green's new growth will shoot up in several months are for the moment russet-colored. They clump in the water too shallow to cover and look like topknots on carrot-haired kids, or like yarn wigs for clowns. The snow is sparse and couldn't cover them, since the wind keeps the blades in motion more often than not. On the days when it does snow to cover, the topknot tussocks are only knots, only bumps.

Their russet is one of the few strong colors around the pond, and they bulge up like blood blisters. Branches seem to be blood-filled too: as I look up through the limbs of deciduous trees, their pattern seems to be veins twigging off into capillaries. The unpigmented sky behind them appears to be the skin just under the surface of which the crisscrossing strands of the webbing that is circulation pulse and trickle. Here too it is the wind that animates, nudging the branches and stirring the clouds into membrane and vessel. I think I'm seeing a magnification of elderly legs, specifically the calf, on which the veins are dilated, tortured, varicose, knotting up under the worn-out integument. My own skin creeps into young bumps with the chilly image.

I walk and jiggle my arms to keep what real blood there is at the pond in motion. I shout out a curse that chimes back at me twice, which serves me right. It doesn't do to curse winter, since winter has no need to be liked. Winter, like the best teacher, is not a buddy but rather a disciplinarian who makes demands but makes them justly, makes them of everyone. Winter is out for respect, not affection.

I stomp on the ice to see if it groans, then step gingerly across it as if skeptical of tests. I make no habit of ice walking, much prefer the circumference in winter, will cross only when, as now, what I want is directly across from me. What I want is the stand of common cattail that is another color, even if still brown-toned, and that is another chink in the otherwise pigmentless landscape.

In spring the stand will doubtless be full of muskrats, who will use the stalks for food and home-building. Smaller than the beaver and less skilled, the two have an interesting relationship: muskrats have been observed storing food in the main and secondary beaver lodges, even when there are kits within, and they're thought to enter the lodges to consume leftovers. Their own lodges, built in the marshiest part of ponds, are made of grasses but manage still to be of a construction similar to the beaver's lodge, even if they haven't the same safe and solid look as the beaver's mortared fortress. They are rodents both, but my own opinion is that the muskrat is a derivative, a watered-down creature that is less to write home about. And yet, what I wouldn't give just now to see the laterally flattened tail snake along behind the oval brunette body of a muskrat. They give the impression of being quite companionable.

Up close the cattails are not very handsome. They've lost the sleek brown-velveteen cylinder they are until late fall because a seam has split and they are partway inside out. The beige interior fur spills out and looks tattered or moth-eaten, abused by wind and by birds after seed. They look like woolly untended sheep in need of shearing, or like scarecrows spilling stuffing, abandoned.

I squat against a tree back from the cattail marsh and decide to try and pick up color through the binoculars. Color on a gray immobile day like this is anything that isn't brown for bark or olive for pine needle. Eventually, and seemingly as a reward for patient, feet-numbing concentration, I locate a pack of deer back through the trees. They are redder than the bark and furry

with a winter growth that mostly hides the fact that they are skinny from food scarcity. One forages, kicking back the snow with a foreleg in a stiff-legged sideways motion, then sticks its nose down to munch on the frozen ground cover. Another stretches up to peel bark from one of the younger trees, a tree already stripped up to the point within comfortable reach of an adult deer. Others nuzzle, licking each other's face from lying-down positions. There are no males; they are does and offspring

passing time, blending in with the whites of the rings around their eyes and nose, the under-chin and inside-ear whites that look like snow on branches.

On another day I sat forever in a blind and finally saw wild turkeys. They had become extinct in Massachusetts but were reintroduced in 1959 and are reported to be doing well. That day I saw a single egg-shaped male and a harem of cone-shaped females who pecked relentlessly at the snow, scratching for acorns, while the male strutted back and forth, fanning its tail open wide and rotating it like a radar screen. The females' feathers made elegant capes of speckles and tweeds that impressed me much more than the smashing multicolored fan, which, I'm sorry to say, made me think more of painted cardboard turkeys in the November windows of every elementary-school classroom I have ever seen. But both impressed me for the strange and wiry black tuft of long hair that hangs from the sternum of both sexes as if a talisman, a voodoo shrunken-head amulet worn as if to embody their wildness and thus their remove from the paper decorations of small children. The same wiry hair sprouts out from the creases of gobble-red necks that look enflamed and sinister with disease, but that are of course only regular old wild-turkey necks seen through overpowered field glasses, taken out of context. Those turkeys kept busy for maybe fifteen minutes before the male swaggered off and the deferential females followed with bowed beaks that kept on pecking even in transit.

This day ended early, because of my contentment with having seen the deer, which is another way of saying that it justifies a day to have seen something, anything. Some days are only thirty minutes long, especially if the air is unduly hostile. What I do with the rest of some of those days is to visit the lab of my film-maker colleagues who keep pond water in tanks and jars in a Cambridge basement. We watch microscopic vegetables bloom and reproduce, anticipating the pond by months. They take pictures, I take notes, and we collaborate. Otherwise, I read dozens of books all at once and console myself with the testimony of others that winter is not the season one wishes long life.

The "anything" I've been glad to have as departure points can be truly anything. Once it was a blue jay nipping buds. It was a bright day, and the jay was splendid in soft blues and grays. A slight wind ruffled its slicked-down hair feathers at the crown, and its white breast puffed with air. So pristine, so solemn, the jay couldn't have resembled less the ragged annoyance birds of suburban bird-feeder fame, even though it was in fact vandalizing the tree it perched on. In nature, everything's up for grabs.

I watched four goose-stepping Canada geese one day earlier in winter. There had been a freak snow, and these four were behind a flock of forty southbound migrators by two days. It had snowed in the night, and first thing in the morning I saw them marching in file, actually left-right-lefting it, perfectly synchronized. Well, not quite perfectly if you compare them with a fascist army on parade, but then geese aren't trying to show off but only to locomote through the snow they meant to be ahead of. In fact, fascists miss the point entirely: goose-stepping done by a goose is a last-resort sort of measure. If fascists wanted to imitate majesty, it was flight drill they needed. The four took off and flew as an absolute unit, a sleek and streamlined uniformity that mocked armies everywhere.

Anything one day was really something. I'd had yet to see an otter, and though I honestly wasn't preparing myself to see them skidding down a slide to "The Flight of the Bumblebee" or some other giddy music, I'd have expected to see one at least, since they are a major enemy of beaver kits. When I did see one, it was so close at hand that I imagined momentarily it was after all a Disney otter. It surfaced just in front of me and poked its black patent-leather baby-seal head way out of the water, enough to bring the forelegs up to rest on the ice like a swimmer on a canvas raft. But the ice was slush, and there was no foothold. The otter scrambled, then apparently lost curiosity; it dunked into a dive, and the last I saw was a bit of its vinyl back. The entire event lasted, at the outside, fifteen seconds. It was, however, one of my best encounters.

There's so little humor at the pond in winter that when a counter of ice turns out to be slush, it's enough to laugh about for weeks. I certainly wish there were more. At times I get tired of the sheer beauty of everything at the pond. It seems like a mannequin, arching, aloof, when what I guess I'm wanting is the pal you bring home after school. I'm almost always stunned by the beauty, but then there's the near-simultaneous wish that it weren't so static. For instance, ice forms on twigs in a string of gorgeous cut-crystal beads, each one a prism that plays with the winter light. But flesh would melt them.

Reflections on the first ice of winter, before the first snow, are so clean and clear that it's possible to watch the clouds move across the sky while looking down. The trees are fixed and the water under the ice is still; just the clouds in filamentous wisps or filligree screens or bulkier puffs pass in front of the sun and show up in the mirror the ice is. It's a transfixing sight but nonetheless a disembodied beauty, a sight that has the hollow quality of an echo.

And then the ice goes through its phases, from a silk that is so fine it is transparent, to a gauzy chiffon, to a stiff and watermarked taffeta that you know would rustle imperiously when danced in, to a brocade fit for throne upholstery, to a fur, the ermine cloaks of high church officials, lustrous and pure snow-white. The problem? The problem is the blood is blue. The problem is with ball gowns that are meant to be looked at, never touched. At times the pond has this problem. Its standoffishness is both attracting and unwelcoming. When I get this riffraff feeling and find winter haughty, I leave like a forsaken suitor who has been awed but also bitterly disappointed.

On this kind of day I'll make my way to the lab as well, to shake off the chill by training for spring. One day it happened that there was the perfect antidote to the brilliant vacuity at the pond. Several fairy shrimp had been obtained and were swimming around in a tank of freezing water. They are one-quarter to one inch long, and they swim on their backs with

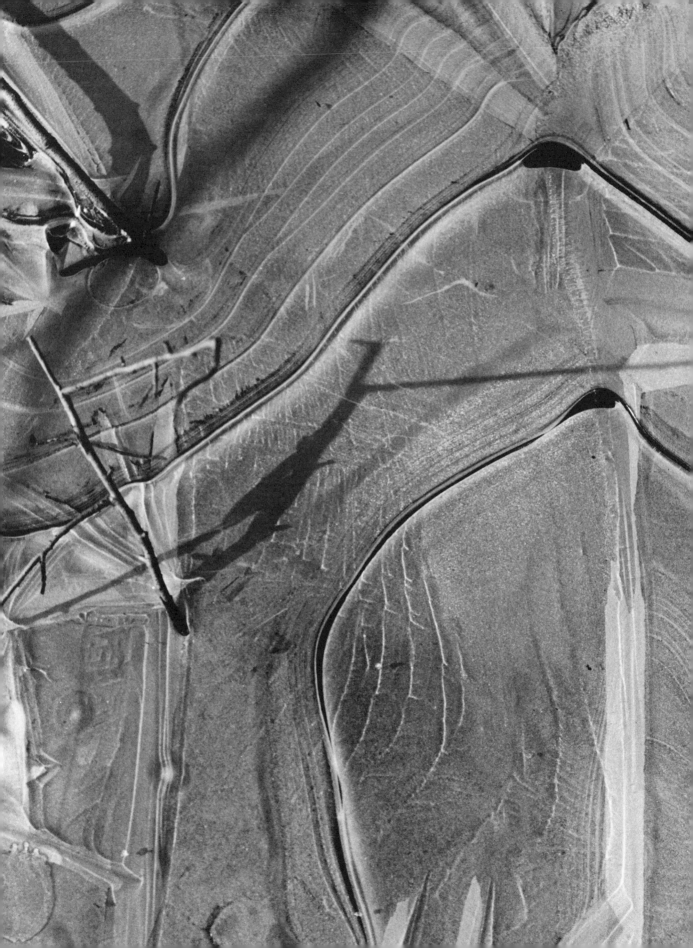

eleven pairs of legs they press against the water in pairs from back to front in order to navigate and draw water over their gills at the same time. Their legs are feathery, and water shimmies through them like wind through grasses. Their heads are shrimplike, and their color, a translucent greenish-pink or pinkish-green, is a gossamer version of the shrimp's. Fairy shrimp is the perfect name for them. The water in their tank is freezing because winter is their season. They lay dormant unfertilized eggs that develop into spiderlike nauplii, then into fairy shrimp, the adult population peaking about as the small pond in which they characteristically live just clears of ice, and declining soon afterward. It is a relief to see at the lab what can't be seen at the pond, and to be reminded that there are, even if small, exceptions to the winter paralysis. To be reminded in fact that there are species who thrive in winter and die off with spring, who put up with the friendly seasons in order to get round to winter again, for whom the cycle reverses itself. The ambidexterity of nature.

No, the genius of it. Winter is a master magician who uses no props, creates simply out of wind an illusion of activity. All you must do if you want to see real magic is to sit and let the wind look like scarves being pulled forever from hats that aren't there. Let the wind stir the landscape as if there were ghosts by the several hundred, browsing. Or, if you find this too eerie, look at snow.

Catch falling flakes on black felt, put it under a microscope, and train high-intensity light on it. Against this background, the crystals all formed on variations of six will jump out at you as they melt before evaporating. The points will look like starfish until you let your mind go, after which they will look like twinkling fanciful jewels for the time it takes to get from semiliteral to completely abstract. You will watch the intricate crystal formations *rushing toward* extinction. The experience is beyond eeriness; it is too far out of reach of the emotions. It generates a total numbness that can only be appropriate to a very few experiences, of which encountering infinity must be another.

Kill

Winter, like a drama, is a three-part affair. First there is the activity, or inactivity, we have been looking at: the iced-over, the dormant, the motion frozen and poised. But when it is not a time for nothing, winter is either a time for breeding, or death.

Beavers breed in late January or early February in the iced-over water that supports their body weight during mating. They pair for life, and there is usually just one parenting couple to a lodge. In the sleeping chamber they will have prepared a bed of grasses and rootlets which the newborn kits will consume soon after their birth. During the average gestation period of 105 days it seems the main activity is waiting.

The northern race of striped skunk, the *Mephitis mephitis hudsonica,* breeds in holes in the ground made by it or by other animals. The females den in groups of eight to ten and remain under cover from December until late spring, mating in late February or early March with the males, who roam throughout the winter. They are believed to be polygamous, which presumes that when a male enters the den it is in order to couple with perhaps the entire community of females.

Otters also are squatters with no fixed abode except during the birthing season, for which time they take over abandoned lodges or dens. Their breeding schedule is interesting in that they breed in January or February, but implantation of the egg is delayed until later in the year, at which point begins the gestation period that lasts for nine to twelve months, ending with the birth in April or May.

The young of the long-tailed weasel also are born in late April or early May, after a greatly varying gestation period of from 103 to 337 days, the variation due to the delayed implantation of the fertilized egg. In snow country the weasel turns white in winter and back to brown in spring. It hunts rodents chiefly but will eat any small animal it can get. The father feeds the young and remains with the family at least until they can care for themselves.

The mink has a weasel-like appearance, is dark brown with a black-tipped tail, but is an excellent swimmer as the weasel is not. The females and males are reported to live in separate dens, the females giving birth after a seven- or eight-week gestation period to a litter of baby mink, who are born naked and blind. The breeding is in late February to March, and the birthing in late April or early May.

The raccoon births at the same time as the mink but mates a little earlier, in late January. It spends the winter in partial hibernation, either alone or in a group, and comes out on warm days to hunt for any of the foods that make up its omnivorous diet. The young are ready at two months to accompany the mother on food hunts.

The point of these examples is to suggest that whereas winter is the sterile season, it is also for most mammals an index of fecundity. Winter hides in the folds of its cloak these unnumbered embryos that are developing, even as winter deepens in hostility, into a multiplicity of fetuses that will, with the thaw, be born into the world.

But then it is necessary to invert the proposition once again, because this promise of fruitfulness is very often not kept, and the reason again is the harshness of winter. These mammals just mentioned to illustrate a developing plenitude are predators and/or prey, and never more urgently than in winter.

Fox droppings contain the hair and bones of field mice, and otter feces are deposits of fish scales. Weasels drag muskrats from their shelters and splatter the snow with their blood. Owls dive after rabbits and snap the life from them. Predators on beaver adults may be Eastern coyotes, bobcats, or stray dogs; in wilder settings, wolves, bear, and mountain lion. Every species hunts to catch whatever it can, and females pregnant with young provide a succulent bonus for their predators.

What I have long wondered is why woods are so rarely littered with bones. When you think of the thousands of corpses and

the many thousand inedible parts left behind when the bottom of the pecking order finishes picking over the remains, it's a bit bewildering that the snow doesn't melt to uncover a wall-to-wall calcium carpet. You'd think the woods would look like a storeroom for vertebrae and collarbones and teeth and nails. What does fighting tooth and nail mean, if not to the death after which there remain only tooth and nail? I have never seen a tooth or a nail on a walk through the woods. I found once the collarbone of a deer, and once the backbone of a fox. In the South perhaps I'd understand. I'd assume that the kudzu which grows a foot every day would be a likely swallower of traces. But Massachusetts? We have no such creepers here. Ground cover in New England is, like everything else here, sedate and well mannered.

What happens, of course, is that the earth absorbs what's left the way a bulb retrieves its nutrients from the stalks it sends up, from which store it will continue to sprout the following year. The needy soil sucks back into itself the calcium-phosphate fertilizer the animal bones are, so that the reason the indigestible remains don't remain is simply that nature has no remainders. Water loosens the soil and gravity does the rest. Snow covers the bones, but the thaw is what buries them.

This way the last word is the earth's, which satisfies its needs without fanfare or violence, taking in and making use of the leftovers of the chain of creatures that feed on corpses. And this way, the fight isn't tooth and nail. A fight to the finish is only another way of saying dust to dust.

But then one afternoon, when it was a sinister mid-February day anyway and when the cold light made the landscape seem to have been tinted with urine, I came upon the carcass of a doe that had been pregnant until its womb was broken into and emptied. The desolation of the place had been getting on my nerves all day, and this was the final outrage. THOU SHALT NOT KILL blazed out of me as if I had invented the admonition. A frozen web of red strands matted in the hide and was what was left of the placenta. The womb, as if it were a Pharaoh's tomb, had been robbed of treasure.

41   Kill

And one of the doe's forelegs had been taken off its hinges, and one of its hind legs stripped of flesh. The head was twisted on its neck to suggest the worst: that the deer had been felled by dogs that didn't know how to kill, and that the deer, in an adrenaline shock, had watched itself being eaten alive. The busiest tracks around the corpse were indeed dog tracks.

The coat had been torn back from the lower ribs for access into the chest cavity, but it still fit snugly over the upper ribs. Too snugly, in fact. The doe had been possibly close to starvation and would have had the look, alive, of another luckless doe I'd seen, who was both heavy with pregnancy and emaciated.

By late winter the deer have little left in the way of browse. They are reduced to eating the twigs of hardwoods, of which it takes around seven and a half pounds a day to sustain one adult. The tips of twigs are nowhere near as nourishing as other browse long since depleted, and the deer become dopey with hunger, edgy, and easily threatened. They gather in larger and larger herds and live in clearings called deer yards, for protection, but the problem is that when one is startled, all will tend to flee crazily, burning precious calories needed for sustenance. It mustn't be too difficult to cull the weakest, bringing down the exhausted prey by grasping a leg and tearing its tendon. Dogs hunt in mixed-breed packs by day and often leave behind an ample feast for those other animals who haven't homes to return to and who find the winter living meager.

On another carcass I once watched eagles scavenging. Counting both golden and bald, I saw at a time as many as ten eagles dancing around the dead deer. They had come for the season, probably from Canada and the coast of Maine, where they nest, to look for food. I was in a blind and watched them through binoculars.

The deer had been dropped on the ice over the pond, and so the eagles were less nervous than they might have been had it been in the woods. But the wind caused apparent problems, whipping across the ice as it did, and the results were quite comical. Both the golden and the bald looked like vaudeville shufflers in baggy pants, this effect created by the wind ruffling the leg feathers. They jerked their wings to help hold them steady, and their feet danced around for footing. Once it was found, they lurched their heads forward and swiftly pulled off plugs of flesh, or they tugged, rearranged their enormous feet for better leverage, and tugged again until the hunk was torn free. They never ceased moving their heads, though the goldens seemed less uneasy than the balds. Both turned their heads in an amazing pivot that went past profile and behind it; again the balds were more striking here, rotating their snowy knob heads along the crease of what looks like a rickrack border between the white and the rich brunette body feathers. The iris of the eye appears clear and is far more piercing, chilling even, than colors are. The scaly yellow foot has hooklike black claws at its tips. The eagle is a mandarin.

But still, no matter how absorbing it can be to study animals eating one another, something in me needs to rebuke nature. Annie Dillard suggests in *Pilgrim at Tinker Creek* that the problem may be less with the offending evil and more with the issue of our having emotions. She says: "Although it is true that we are moral creatures in an amoral world, the world's amorality does not make it a monster. Rather, I am the freak." True enough. And yet still, sometimes I can't put up with it.

That February afternoon was one time, and I haven't since been able to keep the sight out of my mind. The eviscerated pregnant doe clings to the undersurface of my unconscious as a snail clings to the underside of the pond's surface membrane. It seeps into dreams and clouts me often, awake, with an image I close my eyes against still, seasons later.

One tries not to anthropomorphize, but vainly. Something about the twist in the neck encourages me to imagine that what was in the eyes was horror. I imagine, altogether without basis in science, both that I am the deer and the deer is me. Of course Disney exploited this interchange with *Bambi,* and of course, like probably every other child in the country, I was that orphan as much as that sad little fawn was me. Now, grown up,

I'm the doe. And the doe, who's had the ghastliest crime perpetrated against her—belly slashed and a midterm fetus ripped out and eaten, or eaten while within her, the placenta either way slurped out, leaving hardly a trace—and the doe is me.

Better it would be to have let the doe lie there and not imagined anything. Better to stop the data coming in from nature's every quarter, to stop the pain that is the interface of belief in the Ten Commandments (to put it simply). Better? No, not better. The best and only thing to do is somehow to accommodate the chaos, make a peace with it. For evolution depends on the routine violence of unspeakable numbers of creatures killing. Evolution's facilitator is death.

And evolution is, it goes without saying, what got us where we are today. Of the several billion years of some form of life on earth, humans have evolved over a period of only a few million. How so extraordinarily fast? Our intelligence, one facet of which is our feelings, acts as a kind of gill through which an exchange with the outside world takes place. What makes us "superior," what has allowed us to develop with this unheard-of rapidity, is precisely our capacity to take in sensations and make something of them, make choices around them.

Diversity depends on death, as new growth for its chance to improve things depends on a cleansing destruction by fire of a forest. Change, that thing we live for as if it were a synonym in its every meaning for vast improvement, depends on idols being smashed to smithereens. We are capable of accommodation.

I'm not the doe, and the doe isn't me. Should my belly be slashed and an unborn eaten before my living eyes, my eyes would tell of more than horror, and I'd not be likening my killer to a dog gone wild for an afternoon. The pregnant doe was killed not out of a violation of good by evil, but out of a lack of concern for, even knowledge of, either. If I have to make like Moses over this one dead body, well, that's my problem. *Thou Shalt Not Kill* is what goes for us. Whoever said it must go for them?

Succession

When a season is in its peak, there is a self-containment about it that makes for difficulty in remembering that the season is only one of four. When the pond is full of winter, for example, and that season's extremities are isolated from the cycle of which they are part, the pond with its ice and snow seems complete, and no trace of fall and no promise of spring can impose themselves by interjection. These climaxes announce the perfectly obvious: that all the rabbits are out of the hat.

But when all the rabbits are out of the hat, the show is over. What enthralls us is the development, the deepening in intensity, the movement toward, more than the reaching of, the fullness. We want never to let the magician go offstage. We beg for an encore. We need to know there's at least one more rabbit we haven't yet seen. We want the show to go on all year.

So when the seasons overlap and jostle one another as a riptide in the collision of current and countercurrent, the audience cheers. We love nothing more than a snowstorm in May, or a day at the beach in October. We prefer spring and fall to summer and winter, partly because they lessen the intensity and monotony of deep heat or cold, and partly because they're the uncertain seasons, the unreliables. Anything goes.

And so if the between seasons, spring and fall, keep us on the edge of our seats with expectation, even more so do the more subtle betweens. Between spring and summer, summer and fall, between fall and winter, winter and spring. These betweens seem to teeter on brinks and walk tightropes. We hold our breath; we are fully in the power of the impresario.

My own favorite is between winter and spring, when the sun just begins to warm, when it is no longer a metal disk in the sky but a maker of puddles.

The crystal beads of ice on the branches melt into tears and weep themselves out of existence. There are trickles every-where, drawn by gravity down to the pond. The frost heaves itself up and out of the soil as if magnetized by the sun that melts it. It seeps back in, or runs off, or sits there waiting either

to run off or seep in. The earth is soggy and squishes when stepped on, and makes a sound as if the topsoil were the sole of a wet tennis shoe. The ice is not safe to walk on; its top and bottom layers are turning to slush, and it shrinks back from the banks it latched onto and floats like a scum.

This is not by any means the most attractive time of year, in fact there's little dignity in it. It's the moment when the actor has removed only half of the makeup and looks homely, streaked and bruised, instead of theatrical or, once it's all off, normal. One wonders how the pond will accommodate all the water, and whether the earth will drown and rot. Of course the pond will and of course the earth won't, but one wonders still. For one thing, the trees don't seem capable of doing what they do once winter loses its grip on them. Still they look like sleepwalkers poised at the top of the stairs, held back by some force that is slightly more awake than they are.

What trees do when the time is right is literally to re-create themselves by plunging as if down a staircase into the business of spring. The most dramatic figures I've seen on trees come from *Pilgrim at Tinker Creek:* that every year a tree remakes 99 percent of its living parts; that water, up to a ton of it a day, climbs up a tree at a rate of 150 feet an hour; and that a large elm "in a single season might make as many as *six million* leaves." Well. And that's what I mean when I say that the trees don't seem up to it in that between time, between the mute season and the moment of activation. (If activation is the word. It might more likely be detonation.) They don't look like a charge the sun is going to explode, and they certainly don't appear capable of turning water into wine.

But it's all there, and one has simply to wait. The sun, melting the ice down into sheet cakes and down again into cubes, is releasing the nutrients that will be kept from being swept downstream by the beaver dam. A billion overwintering eggs, or more or less, will one of these days be set off by the sun. The single-cell plant life likewise. Winter is receding and at the same time yielding to spring, acceding to succession.

What succession means depends on the context. For ecologists it means the adaptation of organisms to a changing ecosystem. For forest land at Temper Brook, succession is woods fashioned into a pond. For the stones pulled from the soil and piled into walls, it is subsequent use by beavers in building dams and lodges. For farmers it is technology's squeeze, and crops traded in on a lucrative life.

Mill Village had at least one mill down by the old stream. It rises up now above a ten-foot waterfall at a point on the brook that the beavers haven't touched yet. The giant stone foundation sits like a castle on the Rhine, on antique haunches. For the old mill, succession is passage from use to disuse. It is either progress or its opposite.

What succession means for the seasons is layering. As geological progression can be traced in the walls of a canyon, the seasons can be seen in traces on the landscape. A season sits on top of its predecessor, and covers, but is like cellophane at first, developing opacity and acquiring density over time. Eventually it too will show through in the overlap of the following season's cellophane. One succeeds to the next and next involuntarily.

So: two kinds of thinking need to be done about succession. One has to do with finding parts, and the other with losing parts in the whole.

In Thornton Wilder's *Our Town,* Rebecca reports to George the address written to Jane Crofut on a letter written by the minister of her church in the town she was in before she came to Grover's Corners. It begins: "Jane Crofut; The Crofut Farm; Grover's Corners; Sutton County; New Hampshire; United States of America."

When George remarks that he finds nothing remarkable in that, Rebecca tells him it goes on: "Continent of North America; Western Hemisphere; the Earth; the Solar System; the Universe; the Mind of God."

And that's what succession is: thing incorporating thing. Succession is sequence. The Mind of God succeeds it all. Ironically, of course, Grover's Corners and the other traced-in town called Mill Village traded for their existence on values that have to do with durability, with endurance. The ethic is self-sustenance and self-containment, with productivity the facilitator. Trouble is, with the land grown unsuitable for row or forage crops, what's to produce? And eventually Mill Village exists entirely in the Mind of God.

A Sioux would say the white man's kind of village dies because of its square corners, its box buildings on right-angled lots. Disharmony, Sioux call it. "It is a bad way to live, for there can be no power in a square." The old Sioux named Black Elk, whose observation this is, goes on:

You have noticed that everything an Indian does is in a circle, and that is because the Power of the World always works in circles, and everything tries to be round. . . . The sky is round, and I have heard that the earth is round like a ball, and so are all the stars. . . . The sun comes forth and goes down again in a circle. The moon does the same, and both are round. . . . The life of man is a circle from childhood to childhood, and so is everything where power moves.

Succession is circles within circles, wheels within wheels. In a way, what the beaver has made of Mill Village is a circle out of a square. Operating precisely on the same ethic as the former residents of Mill Village, the beaver created egg-shaped ponds within and around which come into existence more spherical cells than could even be approximated. And all of this is kept in motion by prey and predator spinning on the circle of the food chain, eating and being eaten, decomposing and being born.

But beavers, like Sioux and like farmers, can have their circle broken by overharvesting or by bacterial infection in the form of tularemia. They are sacred, if at all, only momentarily, like farmers and like Indians.

Le tems s'en va, le tems s'en va, ma Dame, Las! Pierre de Ronsard wrote that in the sixteenth century, but Ecclesiastes said it better, earlier. "A generation goes, a generation comes, yet the earth stands firm for ever."

Stands firm, but is always changing. The beaver, later on when the living isn't easy, will move on or die out, surrendering its pond fields to meadow and eventually back to forest. The land evolves and is capable of contradiction.

For instance, land that once was the Fertile Crescent now is desert. Arable land is being desertified at a present rate of fourteen million acres a year. The Sahara moves southward, every year claiming sixteen miles more, and all the efforts of governments and humanitarian groups to stop the sterile sand from consuming cropland are thus far futile. Already 43 percent of the earth is arid or semi-arid, and predictions are that in another twenty-five years one-third of all the world's productive land will be lost. The desert spreads—imagine sixteen miles a year in terms of the community you live in—like a viciously contagious disease. Shall we all, like Babylon, expire?

But that's what succession is. Seasons revolve from way-of-being to way-of-being, compensating for each other's failings, making contributions of their own, then disappearing. Mill Village and the Temper Brook pond exist momentarily in the Mind of God, let us say. What *endures* in the Mind of God is more likely the fact that one succeeds the other. Seasons exist, the cycle endures.

Some days I imagine the earth as a year, with season rotations going on all over the place but never in unison. Sometimes I can broaden the image and think of the universe as a year. I can hear the universe being sung, and it is a round, the chorus in distinguishable but overlapping units. It makes either a tuneless cacophony or a finely wrought sound web, depending on my ability to concentrate. It is always awesome.

And those days when the song is sweetest, when I am lying about at the pond and can hear all the notes in harmony with the tunes that are in the air, which I think of as waving in from outer space, it kills me to know that this doesn't endure. But the fact that it doesn't, and that instead the universe is forever being remodeled, is also what I live for.

Father, paint the earth on me.
Father, paint the earth on me.
Father, paint the earth on me.
A nation I will make over.
A two-legged nation I will make holy.
Father, paint the earth on me.

Black Elk recites this song the Ogalalas sing while they dress and are painted for the Horse Dance. The earth is holy. The way to make a nation holy is if it can be made to harmonize with the earth, if the two can be one.

Our technological culture, on the other hand, tends to view its relationship to nature in terms of either acquiescence or dominance. We submit to earthquake, avalanche, and tidal wave because we must. But I think we resent it. We hate to yield and love to subdue. I think we are never happier than when we're performing the acts of God.

And yet, we do love a show. I said we prefer the off-balance seasons, and here's, I think, why. If we take risks and succeed at them, we gain support for the concept that we are holy men and women. When a river rages but can't displace us, we take it as proof. But the desert is spreading in spite of our efforts, and probably will continue to spread even when we get around to getting our best effort out. It's all vastly bigger than we can conceive of. Already there's a cellophane layer being laid over us, out in space. It may take a millennium before it grows opaque enough to obscure us, but it will, eventually.

Father, paint the earth on me.

March is the pivot month. Winter's grip begins to slip, and spring, which is not yet in place, begins to gather its forces. March is both part of the cycle and the moment it is.

Where the stream runs through the pond, the ice is worn thinnest first. The water rubs against the underside of the ice and creates diamond-shaped holes through which is visible the blackest water. These seeps chain together to indicate the path of the water; eventually they will make a necklace of what looks like onyx.

But up close, before the thaw has progressed much, each seep is a little spectacle of its own. A thin transparent shelf of ice borders the seep, and the water running under it, which now doesn't touch it from beneath, manages to look like currents of light running along tracks. The edges become bands of a sort of neon light, as if for lettering, as if for making an announcement.

The silver and black of the seep stand out from the more ordinary pastels that characterize the thaw's first stages, the pastels that are contained, because all colors make white, in the milky ice. There are faint traces of blues that reflect the still watery sky, but the blues are dull and grayish with a metallic edge. There are orangy rusts that hint of the beef-bouillon color the water is, filled as it is with the debris of decomposed vegetation. The ice is disintegrating. Its parts are showing.

Since it's too warm to snow, it rains and rains. The swelling of the pond breaks up the ice, and the ice bits jam together flake on flake as if making minerals of themselves, or as if they were fluted fungi. The larger clumps break away and twirl in the current like ballerinas, then bash and are fixed in other wholly transitory constructions. But they can only go so far. The dam is like a prison guard.

Farther down the stream, beyond the last dam, the breakup has another character altogether. The ice has somewhere to go

and seems to hurl itself downstream, spiraling uninhibitedly, whirling dervishly. It dives off the ledge and drops over the fall as if to free itself of its cumbersome casing by shattering it on the ready rocks. It drags along whatever it can: branches, logs, roots, stones, silt kicked up from the bottom, soil pulled away from the banks. The cavalry fleeing.

It's amazing to me that this is the same water in both places, and I am entirely respectful of the beaver as engineer. The dams contain all but what amounts to trickles, penning in the ice so that when the melt is achieved the nutrients will have been released into the pond itself, rather than given over to the seaward flow that goes and goes until it has lost itself in the salt. The beavers are expert conservationists.

And I learn from them also the meaning of water over the dam. We use the expression in soothing hard feelings, in order to convey forgiveness, to let go of grievances: water over the dam is water gone away, forgotten, shrugged off. But water that goes over the dam is water lost, is water irretrievable, is water that goes off to work elsewhere. Water over the dam does not evaporate, as we seem to think. It spirals fiercely, it rushes headlong, it charges off with the fury. Water over the dam is precisely what succession is all about.

Spring

In our yards and gardens, spring means crocuses peeping through snow and opening boldly, showing off their cups of saffron. Spring means exhibitionistic tulips, feathery-lush forsythia, bellowing trumpets of daffodil, nectary narcissus, spiky iris in swaddling buds blooming into velvet bows, springy curlicues of hyacinth the colors of claret, blueberry, or dandelion wine. It means the prancing robin redbreast and earthworms wrenched from between the blades of chartreuse grass. And fruit trees breaking into flower as if into song. It means twigs becoming parasols and branches umbrellas and trees themselves huge tarpaulins. Spring means balloons of color coming up from the earth and ascending.

The pond's spring is dim by comparison, and its balloons are barely visible. The colors are muted and shadowy, subtle ones. Spring doesn't burst upon the pond with bugle fanfare and ostentation; it's more discreet. The changes that count are microscopic.

Billions of years ago, in what was doubtless the boldest evolutionary stroke ever, green algae "invented" sexual reproduction. Now there are over thirty thousand species of algae, ranging from the one-cells to the giant kelp which is capable of growing to two hundred feet. The algae can be either aerial, terrestrial, or aquatic. If aquatic, they are one of two types: benthos (shore and bottom algae) or plankton (free-floating). The algae are judged to be responsible for 90 percent of all the earth's photosynthesizing.

Therefore, when spring breaks upon the pond what it signals is the readiness of the water to support all the varied forms of life that depend on it. Algae have been busily transforming six molecules each of carbon dioxide and water into six of oxygen, which they discard, and one of glucose, which they convert into ATP, the fundamental agent of all cell actions and growth processes. Light is the facilitator, the energy source that fuels the exchange. Without light, the plant world would do as it does at night, taking oxygen in and releasing carbon dioxide. With the retreat of the ice that reduced the light source, the

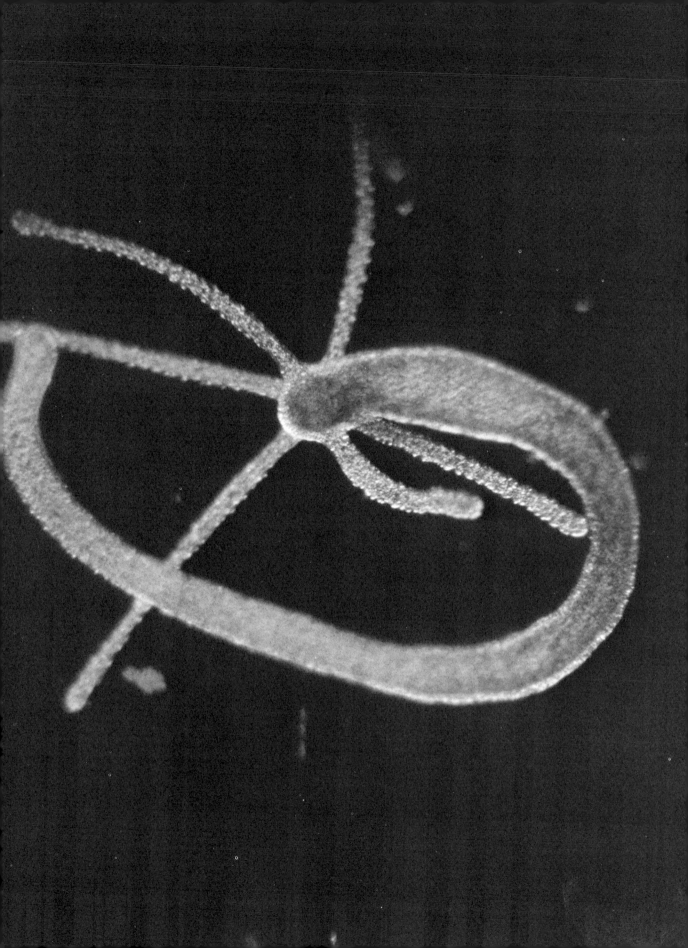

daylight hours provide a bounty of by-product oxygen. When the algae ascend to the water's surface it is on bubbles of the oxygen of their own production. The rise of plankton at the pond is what spring is: breath, and lots of it.

The microscopics under glass make a rain of shapes. They look like what they are, simple-celled miniature vegetables. The hydra is a member of the phylum *Coelenterata,* which includes all jellyfish. It is formed of little columns with a circlet of octopuslike tentacles that sting to paralyze prey. Highly specialized protozoa called Trichodina live on the tentacles but are apparently unaffected by their sting. It is assumed that they keep the tentacles clean of silt in exchange for food. The green hydra, which at one-eighth inch long is much littler than the white, takes its color from a planktonic alga called *Chlorella,* which lives in the tissue of hydra and provides food and oxygen for its host.

One doesn't see all of this, of course, but the fact that the hydra is microscopic doesn't mean it's not complex. The hydra is capable of sexual reproduction and can carry itself to the undersurface of the water on an air bubble formed at the tip of the foot, which grip the foot will then transfer to the surface film. On the other hand, however, the hydra will be consumed by something else that exists for us only by the power of magnification.

Here are more examples of what is going on behind the scenes. *Volvox* are microscopics that are called either algae, because they photosynthesize, or animals, because they can subsist on dead protozoa. Each *Volvox* is round and spins like a globe, as if to display its chlorophyll stones of jade that are actually daughter cells the *Volvox* will burst with.

Named for Pandora, the first mortal woman in Greek mythology, *Pandorina* are similar to *Volvox* but smaller, and most people call them algae. *Pandorina* spin and have daughters within their watery gelatinous envelopes that function as sheaths and look like emerald bracelets.

Daphnia are a species of water flea. As one looks through the transparent casing, one sees what looks like watchworks keeping track of fractions of seconds. When pregnant, the *Daphnia* seem to be beanbags filled with bright-green jitterbugging daughters.

The ostracod is a handsome down-covered pod that looks like a bivalve and has antennae that stick up like periscopes and are used in locomotion. Each averages only a millimeter in length and, except for those living among algae, which are green, the ostracods are brown, orange, and violet in color. They can live under the ice and will swim around in the pond all winter.

The *Stentor* is pear-shaped and bluish green, with whisker-like cilia on its broad end. To navigate, the *Stentor* uses its narrow end as an elastic foot or head that can extend and be retracted. *Spirogyra* are filamentous algae, threads of indefinite length, within each cell of which is a vivid green spiral. In the center of each cell is a milky iridescence, the opalescent nucleus. The *Spirogyra* are both uniquely lovely when seen through a microscope and one of the commonest of the green algae.

Diatoms flourished a hundred million years ago. Meaning "cut in two," the diatom is formed in two halves, like the top and bottom of a box. And each diatom has its own etching pattern, which acts as a prism to focus light rays on its chlorophyll molecules, enabling the diatom to operate far down in the water without its photosynthesizing power being reduced. Diatoms multiply so fast that they can double their population in a day. Under microscope they look like luminescent wands.

Other plants which are vastly more visible, but still minute, are also beginning to reproduce into the warming water. The freshwater sponge releases the tiny spherical overwintering eggs called sponge gemmules into the water from out of their resting places deep within the sponge. Each gemmule had contained enough nourishment to see the egg through the winter; in March or April the fertilized egg escapes through a hole in the gemmule, and takes off.

Duckweed is common to ponds, budding to reproduce and massing to show up on the surface as thousands of green sequins. It has no true leaves or stem, but the thallus, the body of the plant, is called the leaf. The roots simply dangle, if dangle isn't too large a word for something that is a quarter-inch long.

Wolffia, a member of the duckweed family, sink to the bottom in autumn and rise again in the spring when their supply of starch grains has been used up. They are rootless but do produce flowers, and are in fact the smallest flowering plant there is, with a thallus that is just one millimeter long.

The important thing to keep in mind is that once the ice retreats and the signal for spring is given, what is most vital is exactly that which we are incapable of seeing: the infinitesimals photosynthesizing, turning what looks like water into an oxygen broth. And all because of what looks like jade or emerald under the microscope, because of the wonder pigment chlorophyll.

Let this have its own paragraph: the chlorophyll molecule that absorbs the red, orange, and blue rays of the sun and uses this radiant energy in the production of sugar and oxygen is related very closely to the hemoglobin molecule. Red blood and green chlorophyll have but one difference, which is that the central atom of the 136 atoms in a molecule of hemoglobin is iron, and the equivalent atom in chlorophyll is magnesium. All the other 135 atoms are exactly similarly placed around the central atom of either iron or magnesium. It is wonderfully fitting: we can think without being melodramatic of the plankton bloom as the pond's transfusion of healthy blood. We can see the massing plankton that literally coagulate on the surface film as its source, as its lifeblood.

The dangling-rooted duckweed that divides to produce up to 84,000 plants per square meter provides a habitat for hydras and rotifers in its rootlets, and desmids, diatoms, and blue-green algae amidst its stems. Duckweed provides protection for the tiny watermeal plants which would otherwise be blown ashore.

It photosynthesizes cleverly, arranging its chloroplasts vertically in strong light and horizontally in weak light. We can think of the duckweed, keeping in mind that chlorophyll is the pond's hemoglobin, as a capillary-rich pulsing circulatory system, or a blood bank.

Yet all we see is the green pond scum that the current carries, that the wind blows into the pond's alcoves. It seems a measly equivalent to the rambunctious splashiness spring is in our yards and gardens, but isn't. Isn't.

American toad mating call

In addition to the microscopic vegetables, there are other near invisibles that crowd the warming water and give spring its name.

The eggs of the great pond snail are hatching into what look like tiny yellow hardhats, the developing shell not yet enclosing the vibrating transparent innards. The mantle is the tissue that lines the shell and creates either a specialized cavity, a lung, or specialized folds, gills. This makes for the distinction between operculate, gilled, or pulmonate snails. In the pulmonates, the air-filled lung provides the buoyancy needed for crawling on the underside of the surface film, and for hanging there by clinging with the foot, or head, that extends beyond the shell. The snail is a gastropod, which means "stomach-footed."

Frog eggs are bubbles around little brown ridged tongues that lick and flap in spasms that give the appearance of a tadpole doing isometric exercises. The froggy pulsing in the throat begins now and will continue throughout the tadpole's development into lung-breathing frog.

The most evocative insect in its pre-adult stages is the phantom midge. On the hind end of the larva is a transparent finned tail that is composed of fine bristles and that acts as a rudder. The phantom midge larvae propel themselves vertically in the water by the rapid compression of the hydrostatic organ on either end. The larva population declines in early summer when the phantom midge pupates. The pupa hangs right side up suspended from a pair of breathing tubes that look like horns, or antlers, and that enhance the impression the pupae give of being miniature Vikings, or giraffes. It emerges from its pupal case after a grotesque writhing to shed it, then dries off and flies away.

Mosquitoes also go through the complete four-stage metamorphosis: egg, larva, pupa, adult. Rafts of eggs hatch into larvae which hang upside down, two breathing tubes extending from the abdomen to pierce the surface film for air. They pupate in the water, the breathing tubes extending now from the thorax, then break out of their floating pupating cases, balance there, getting ready, then take off into airborne adulthood. If they make it that far.

The dragonfly nymph is a voracious feeder that snaps up its prey by means of a mask, the labium, hooked on the end, that folds up under the head and shoots out to snag food. It eats an assortment that includes mosquito and phantom larvae and tadpoles, and one can watch food being ingested through the transparent head covering, bite following bite from mouth to

stomach. The dragonfly's first year, at least, is spent in this form, living on or near the bottom of the pond and breathing by means of contractions in the abdomen that pump water in and out of the anus and over the tracheal gills that line the rectum. The nymphs may molt up to fifteen times as the complex eye develops new lenses, as the antennae gain new joints, and as wing pads appear. The molts are facilitated by a molting fluid that forms between the outer skin and the new one and that acts as a lubricant for the shed.

When the dragonfly nymph is ready for its metamorphosis into adult, it emerges from the water onto a stem and anchors itself with twelve hooks. The final nymphal skin splits beginning at the thorax, but the dragonfly doesn't free itself of it until after a motionless period of fifteen minutes or so, during which time the wings are hardening. It may take five hours before the dragonfly's wings are pumped completely full of blood and lowered into their horizontal positions in relation to the body. It is common in late spring to see a shed case and next to it the adult gradually pumping up its miraculous veined wings, readying itself for its comparatively short life in the final phase of its three.

Another insect which has an incomplete, three-stage metamorphosis is the mayfly. The nymph has fanlike tracheal gills that are semi-opaque but veined, and that look like pressings between two sheets of rice paper in the shape of leaves caught up by breezes. The water flows over the gills as air over wings. The nymph spends the winter eating, underwater, and emerges in the spring in is sub-imago adult stage, which lasts up to twenty-four hours. Then the exocuticle is cast from the whole body, including the wings, and the mayfly is in the imago stage, the final adult form in which it has only the atrophied remains of a mouth and stomach. The mayfly adult is unable to eat.

The caddis-fly adult lives only a few days, at most thirty. Its wings are a mothlike dusty yellowish-gray, and it is mostly active around the pond at dusk, lapping fluids for food since it has no mouthparts for chewing. It is the larval stage of the caddis that is interesting. What happens is that the jellied egg case containing up to a thousand caddis eggs swells and liquefies during rains, and raindrops carry the hatched young deeper underwater. The larva secretes a "glue" and builds a casing for itself of leaf or stick bits or grains of sand. On stout forelegs it creeps along the pond bottom, dragging the open-ended cylindrical case at a 45-degree angle, feeding either on algae or small plants, or on other insect larvae, worms, and tiny crustaceans. To pupate, the caddis-fly larva spins a cover for both ends of the tube and, locked inside, changes into its pupal form. After a period of several weeks, the pupa breaks out of the case by biting itself free, swims to the surface, crawls onto a stem, and changes in about twenty minutes into its less sophisticated short-lived adult form.

The point again, as with the algae, is that spring at the pond is not at all subdued or retarded, even if the fact is that a late-April day at the pond offers little in the way of visible signs. We have to measure differently, take someone else's word for it, or spend, as I did, hours in labs watching the development in isolation-chamber tanks of ripening infinitesimal fruits and cannibalistic insect minutiae. Spring is this: the emphatically unbarren, the dexterous, the charged, the promiser.

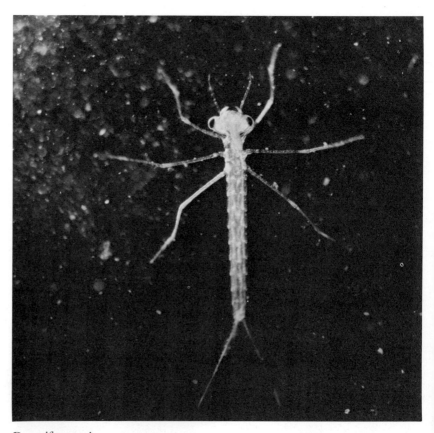

Damselfly nymph

Eventually of course, because spring would have to be called something else if it weren't at some point a coil sprung open, eventually there are visible signs.

The fat buds on trees pop open one overnight, opening into lime-colored parachutes that go from heavily creased to creaseless in no time at all.

The skunk cabbage that appeared through the mud as yellow-streaked purple knots when the trees were still in bud are winding open now into green spiraling leaves that unfurl, as if each leaf were a rolled-up flag. They measure along the center vein up to a foot and a half in late April, and they will keep growing.

Fiddlehead ferns also grow in wet places, sending up new knobs each year from their subterranean stems, the rhizome. First they look like white furry embryos, then, as they develop out of their squeezed-tight fetal positions, the fibrous downy covering is less marked. They grow in clumps of six or eight with one or two pale-green fiddleheads outdistancing the others by as much as 100 percent. To me they look like llamas.

The reason the fiddleheads stay coiled is because the lower portion of the leaf consistently grows more rapidly than the top does. And while this is an arrangement that is unique to the fern, the principle has a more general application. Indeed, it's as if all the pond's vegetation curls around its tips and its blooms until the last minute, uncoiling only because it must. The progress is timidly made; spring does not flaunt its wares.

The yellow Bullhead-lily has a distinctly functional appearance: the blooms look like doorknobs. Three green outer petals shrink back to reveal three yellow coin-shaped petals which open only partially the first day, admitting pollen-laden insects that brush the stigma with pollen from other plants. Only then do the petals open to release pollen from the anthers, only after cross-fertilization has already taken place. Thereafter, from whichever day in May it is until September, the brassy yellow pond-lily sits above the water on rubbery stem. The white

water-lily with pointy petals has much more class but doesn't appear until summer, blooming June to October.

The tight-fisted yellow lilies contrast with the graceful wild iris that grows in shallower water. Its petals are a vibrant purple in delicate arcs, its stalks are slender; each bloom is a miniature bouquet. But the stems of both lily and iris are likely platforms for insect metamorphosis, underlining the fact that spring's blooming isn't just for the purpose of decoration.

Perhaps this is the place to mention plants that live in nitrogen-deficient soil and compensate by consuming insects. The pitcher plant traps insects with the fine hair lining of its "pitcher." The insect drowns in the rainwater accumulated in the bowl and its protein is broken down into a liquid nitrate the plant absorbs. Another insectivorous plant is the sundew, a plant Darwin studied closely to report on the grim details of its feeding: the sundew snares its prey with tentacle-like hairs, on the tip of which is an insect-attracting sticky liquid, and holds the insect tight during the several hours it takes for the plant to close around it. Then the sundew secretes a sort of digestive juice which clogs the trachea of the insect, killing it, and which then renders the insect into digestible parts. After two or more days the leaves reopen; the sundew is back in business again. Why mention it here? Because spring has to do, first and last, with feeding. With gluttony, even.

And this is the real uncoiling. Spring is maybe best described after all by the mention of the gorging that goes on. Fish, reptiles, insects, animals, and plants all feast on each other in "all you can eat" smorgasbord style. A ravenous population seems set to demolish another, but never can. The bounty cannot be inventoried and truly seems bottomless. Feast is a word that understates it.

Snakes eat tadpoles but, as if comeuppance, bullfrogs eat snakes. The classic food web is plankton (producer) eaten by

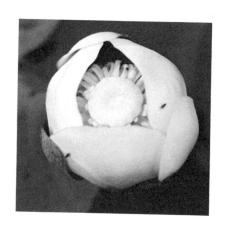

tadpoles (first-order consumers) eaten by bass (second-order consumers) eaten by otters (third-order consumers); and so on up the predator-prey chain until the dead consumer decomposes and its parts are broken down by bacteria and rendered useful to green plants as nourishment. This progression begins underwater in spring and takes in every species: hunger as a centripetal force.

And the plankton bloom now? Now that the season has come through its bit-by-bit revelations and achieved a peak of sorts in frantic feeding, the plankton takes on a new personality. It still shifts from corner to corner, pushed along by the wind the way a mop moves clots of dust from here to there, but it is augmented. Pollen sticks in it, turning it mustardy. Leaves, twigs, grass, and flowerets catch in it, looking like winged creatures in a spider web, making up a design that is superimposed on the netted background. Bubbles cluster and look like ornamental embroidery, eyelet, Alençon, holes to make lace circles to make trails, lace bands. The plankton bloom that was the spring's first sign has become an exquisite mantilla.

Mates

All around the pond all spring and into the summer, the young of the year are being born. Their parents provide what they can in the way of protection, but still and always it is roulette. Nature is a grand casino in which the players gamble their very lives, in which wins and losses are only big. In giving birth, one participates in the greatest game of chance there is: evolution. One plays for better or worse, for keeps, for broke.

Human beings participate in this game of chance too, but there are some important differences. The human female is sexually available at all times, and copulation is not solely for the purpose of breeding. We copulate face to face and are believed to be the only species who does. And it is thought by some, though not by others, that only the human female has orgasms. But what do these differences mean? Are they metaphors, as some see them, for male and female equality among human beings, and inequality among other animals? If they are statements of the joint purposefulness of our mating, do they imply that others mate randomly? Do they literally mean that only among humans is mating a mutual embrace?

Mating is for human beings a long-postponed, deliberate act undertaken thoughtfully, responsibly, and with often elaborate premeditation. In order to account for the incredible speed of human evolution, J. Bronowski asserts in *The Ascent of Man* that this uncommonly careful sexual selection has been our way of augmenting natural selection. We mate according to intelligence, not just according to biological talents, and here Bronowski draws the fundamental distinction between human beings and other species.

But we mustn't assume completely *un*careful selection among animals, or how do we explain Canada geese? The Canadas are those waterfowl with black neck "stocking," gray-brown body lighter at the breast, and striking white throat patch, who are familiar if only twice a year in wedge formation, barking loudly, flying south or north for winter or summer rests. The Canadas live extremely long lives, and they mate for life. And if a Canada loses a mate, it will wait two or three years before taking another.

Even when appearances are that mating for other species is random and anonymous, we can't assume so. I once sat on a porch and watched sea gulls pick through the leftovers between tides. For no reason at all, one gull of the fifty or so had fixed my attention, and I watched it do absolutely nothing for a minute or more. Then another, larger gull jumped that one from behind, grasped with its feet, and began both to pump into and to flatten the first. After, say, ten seconds, the male hopped off and went away. The female readjusted its feathers and simply went back to just sitting there, casting not even an afterthought glance in the direction of the dismounted male. The question is: what did I miss? Gulls have a fine sense of smell; do they not need to look? What did I miss?

There are two points to be made: the first is that none of the rest of nature mates exactly as human beings do, and the second is that it's not the exact opposite either. Our base purposes are identical, in that every species is concerned with adaptation to meet the specific requirements of life. The requirements vary, and so do the methods for adapting.

Now, about the pond and its inhabitants. Since the pond wouldn't exist were it not for the beaver, this is where we begin. But since all we've seen so far of the beaver is its snow-covered dams and lodges, there ought to be a broader introduction.

Beaver tail close-up

The beaver is the largest rodent in North America. It has four gnawing incisors, two uppers and two lowers, that are rather ingeniously adapted to woodcutting. They grow constantly and wear with use to a chisel edge; the back side of the tooth, because it is made of a soft dentine, wears down, whereas the front side, outer-layered as it is with a very strong orange-colored enamel, doesn't. The beaver has lips that can close behind the incisors to keep the mouth free of wood chips and, when the beaver is gnawing underwater, water. In addition there is a lump in its tongue which, when elevated, fits against the palate and blocks passage to the pharynx except when swallowing. The beaver also has a valvular nose and valvular

ears that close underwater, and eyes with transparent membranes that act as goggles.

The head is rather small in relation to the body. While swimming the beaver looks like a barge being drawn by a tug, but on land it is bulky and torso-dominated. Average-size adults weigh around forty pounds, which means that some will weigh seventy or more. The fur, as everyone knows, is luxuriant, a rich highlighted brown. The beaver keeps it waterproofed with an oil manufactured in a pair of oil glands, and rewaterproofs itself each time it leaves the water. In the underfur may live a tiny beetle that is thought to keep the fur clean of debris, which makes for better insulation, and some believe that the beaver also has sensitive guard hairs in its fur, for detecting change in the water current.

Muskrat lodge

The forepaws are adapted to digging, and the webbed hind feet, in addition to functioning as paddles, each have on the second toe a curved double nail which serves as a grooming aid. The tail, a rubbery flat oval with a scaly outermost layer, is a rudder. Other important uses it has are as an aid in balancing on land, as a storage place for body fat, which prevents the nearly hairless tail from freezing, and, when slapped against the water surface, as a warning device to signal the presence of enemies. R.D. Lawrence, a highly reputable naturalist, and author of the book *Paddy,* believes that the purpose of the tail slap is to startle the enemy into giving up its camouflage; and so do I.

The beaver lives in a lodge constructed of mud that is piled up to make a base, on top of which are placed mud-mortared, de-barked branches that are knitted together to form a dome. Once the mud and stick mound has been made, the beaver digs from underwater into the mass and gnaws out a living chamber inside the dome. There may be several tunnels dug to allow access into the chamber from various underwater points. An air vent is made by leaving unplastered with mud a spot in the domed roof's center. Close at hand, underwater, is the stockpiled winter food supply of branches dug into the muddy bottom or weighted with stones.

The mating has taken place in January or February, and the mating pair copulate in the iced-over water in a nearly upright dorsoventral position. When the population is stable, fewer females mate and the litters are smaller; but all will mate, and with larger litters, if the population needs augmenting. A lodge will house the adult pair who mate for life, the yearlings, and the young of the year. The two-year-olds will have been driven from the lodge just prior to the late-spring birthing.

The birth of the two to four kits takes place over a period of up to seventy-two hours. The female folds its tail forward over the belly, and the young are born between the tail and the body. The umbilical cord is held by the forepaws and drawn slowly through the female's mouth.

A kit at birth typically weighs a pound, is furred, and has eyes that are partially open, though its incisors are just an eighth-inch long, and its tail is plano-convex rather than flat. Its grooming nails appear to be functional immediately, and the kit can swim at four to five days, even though it won't leave the lodge until weaned at two months. During this nursing period, in addition to mother's milk it feeds on grasses, twigs, and rootlets, then on branches from the underwater food cache. Born in May or June, it is middle to late summer before the beaver kit sees the world outside the lodge, and vice versa.

Although some say the female drives the male and the yearlings from the lodge for a two-week period during birthing, most think the male is present during the birth, and that together the male and female consume the placenta, drawing it through their mouths as the female did the cord. Either way the male will live with the female and the kits and will share the care of the young. During this period, a microphone lowered into the chamber through the vent picks up whines, hisses, growls, nuzzling noises, and a sort of "talking" sound that is rarely heard outside the lodge, where all communicating is done in high-frequency range. The kits apparently learn their skills from the parenting adults, and by fall they are working members of the community, helping with dam repair, lodge maintenance, and food gathering.

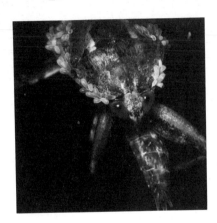
Male giant water bug

But a "nuclear family" setup such as this is uncommon in nature; among species other than mammals it is unheard of. And so let me quickly describe one of the opposite extremes. The giant water bug is two or more inches long and looks like an armored tank. It has a sharp beak with which it pierces prey and through which it secretes a toxin that turns the insides of the prey to soup it sucks out as if through a straw. It leaves behind an empty pouch and nothing more. The female giant water bug attaches its eggs to the back of the male, who will aerate the eggs while swimming for ten days or so. The other reason the eggs are fixed there is that if the male could reach the eggs to eat them it would. As it is, when the young hatch they will eat each other.

And so it goes in nature, where the variations are endless and where the way it is is simply the way it is, no questions asked. A charming description of the way it is is Russell's from his *Watchers at the Pond:* "One snail slid alongside another and inserted his male organ into the female organ of the snail at his side, who in turn inserted a male organ into another snail alongside her—him—and within moments there were several snails copulating passively in a group." No questions asked.

Among fish it is routinely the male who builds the nest and guards the young. Bass males make basin-shaped nests in the shallows, in which one or more females lay eggs stuck together in strings that attach to the stones in the bottom of the nest. The male bass guards the eggs for one or two weeks until they hatch, guards the young for the ten days they remain in the nest, and swims with them after they leave the nest. The sunfish male clears a place for the nest and drives the female into it for egg laying. The sunfish eggs also stick to stones, and the male also stays around to guard them. The stickleback male constructs an igloolike nest by cementing pond material with a specialized substance it secretes. Several females lay their eggs in this nest, which eggs the nest builder fertilizes and watches over.

The female bullfrog is larger than the male and may be eight inches long and a pound in weight. The breeding takes place in

late spring when the water and air have warmed sufficiently, and a female will lay, at night, in a mass on the surface film among vegetation, in a one-by-two-foot area, ten to twenty thousand eggs.

Other frogs mate earlier. One glorious April day I counted thirty-two frogs in a single corner of the pond and watched them puff up and burp out their song, then jump and mount and leapfrog over. It was as if the shallow water boiled with frogs, it was raucous and chaotic, it was mad and also intensely erotic. Eventually I burst out laughing to think that I'd spent thirty minutes watching frogs leapfrog one another without once laughing. The thing is, frogs are just as clumsy at leapfrogging as people are. They press with their front feet on the "shoulders" but never quite hop cleanly over, sliding off to a side instead, as we do. I also laughed, I think, to divert the urge I was feeling to jump in mong them. You have to take my word on how erotic it was.

The red spotted newt is an altogether curious creature. An amphibian, it hatches in the water and spends two to three months as an aquatic larva, developing arms and legs and a granular skin that changes in color from a greenish-yellow to a pale red, with black-bordered red spots in a row on each side of its back, and a yellow belly. It loses its gills and lives terrestrially for one to three years as a hibernating red eft. At the end of the eft stage, during which period the newt is toxic, it migrates back to the pond and in a week develops a tail crest and its smooth adult skin, a drab olive color with black-ringed spots on each side and a black-spotted pale-yellow belly. The adult newt is about three inches long and lives in the water but is air-breathing. Gills once given up cannot be regained.

And curious too are the newt's mating habits. During the spring breeding season, the male newt has a protuberant vent, a large tail crest, and scaly outgrowths on the undersides of the hind legs and on the tips of those toes. It is with these hind legs that the male seizes and grasps the female around the neck, pressing its hedonic glands to the female's snout. With its tail

1

3

2

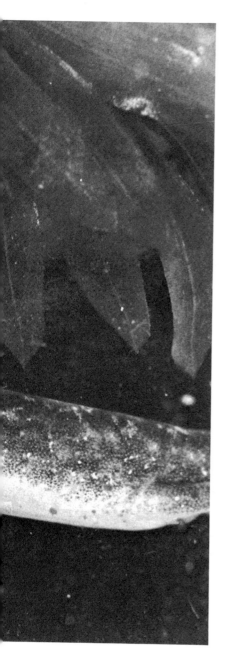

4

1
Newt larva
2
Adult newt
3
Blue spotted salamander larva
4
Blue spotted salamander adult

whipping back and forth, the male directs its scent toward the female's nose until the female is aroused. Then the male dismounts and deposits its spermatophore in front of the female's snout, and the female picks it up with the lips of the cloaca, the single orifice into which open ducts from the reproductive, urinary, and intestinal systems. Fertilization takes place internally, with the eggs laid singly, deposited on a leaf the newt will fold in order to hide the egg. In a month the egg hatches, and the newt goes through its larval and eft stages, coming back to the water to engage in its rigorous breeding rites.

The dragonfly male also clasps the female from above, gripping the female behind the head with the claspers at the end of its abdomen. The female curves its abdomen under and forward and inserts it into the copulatory organ of the male, which is placed far forward on the underside of the abdomen, and into which the male has discharged sperm. While the female collects the sperm, the two fly in tandem, all four wings in synch and genitals interlocking. After several minutes the female straightens itself, and the joined pair drop down for the female to stick the tip of its body below the water surface, depositing fertilized eggs. Then they separate.

Red-winged blackbird males arrive north the end of February, two weeks before the females do. They sit on bare branches, bobbing like gymnasts on barres, and shriek. By the time the females arrive the nesting territories have been apportioned; the female chooses the site and accepts the male that goes with it. Some males have one mate, some two or three. The female is the nest builder with grasses, sedges, or rushes and makes the nest near or over the water. One nest at the pond is in the cavity of a drowned stump, which makes it easily peered into by people like me who travel around the pond on a belly boat fashioned for filming.

The eggs are three to five in number and pale blue streaked with purplish-black. The female incubates them and feeds the young once they are hatched, though the male will assume the

1
Dragonfly
2
Damselfly

1

2

responsibility for food gathering if the female disappears. Which, I gather, is what has happened to the female nesting in the snag, since it is now the male who flies into the nest with dragonflies, worms, and grubs and then flies off again with the "diaper sac," a white pouch of feces the parent carries off in its beak and drops into the water fifty feet or so away from the nest. I have tried to get a close-up of this waste pouch, but each time I peep into the nest all I see is mouth, four wide-open crimson diamond-shaped mouths, and eight bruises where the eyes will be. Anyway, the male screams at me, raging, so I paddle out of there as quickly as possible.

Hawk young get rid of waste by a method that is different from the redwing, and less tidy: the eyas, or nestling hawk, ejects a stream of feces over the edge of the nest. The parent hawk brings its prey to the nest and strips the flesh off for the embryonic-looking eyas, who has a very slight beak and sparse downy feathers, a wobbly head that is dominated by black eye patches. The eyas looks too young to expel its waste over the top, but apparently isn't.

In the heron a parasite develops in the throat and is passed in the feces. Eventually, because it contains a poison, the feces kill the trees the heron nests in, about which I have a theory. The heron's protective coloration is such that its best camouflage is gray-white drowned-out vegetation. It moves in an angular way and is lost against dead branches. So? So its killing the trees in the heron rookery is protection. One barely sees them coming and going, and they are strictly invisible sitting on the nest of whitened sticks. It's as if the heron were specifically protected for beaver ponds.

Ruffed grouse live in the woods around the pond, in summer in clearings, in winter in conifers. Males have splendid feather trains and attract the females with feather displays and by drumming the air with their wings. A drumming male will stand on a log in the same spot every day until it attracts a mate and copulates. The nest is lined with dead leaves and is on the ground in a depression. The young remain for only a short time, then leave the nest to roam with the parents and gather edibles. Grouse are reckless fliers and often crash into branches when they do fly. On the ground, however, they seem to compensate with wit for what they lack in the air. A mother will feign injury to distract a predator away from the young. Not bad.

The problem for every species is how to ensure the survival of the succeeding generation. Some try to beat the odds with numbers, laying tens of thousands of eggs. Some have several nestings in a season. Others rely on extremely careful nurturing, on ever presence, on schooling in caution, and on the fact that the young of these species tend to be very precocious: fully furred, open-eyed, able to run within hours of birth.

One day I watched fox cubs through high-powered field glasses. There were two of them, looking like Siamese kittens with their black paws and ear tips and silvery fur, and acting like puppies, snoozing, scratching, squatting on one another as if inadvertently. Several times a minute, however, they'd jump the couple steps back to the den and disappear into its ditch of safety. It was as if they never forgot for a second the fact of their terrible vulnerability.

Another day I was the unintentional witness, at point-blank range, of a pair of fawns. The birthing month for deer is June, and the date of our collision in the woods was June 14. They were, I suspect, a week old, maybe ten days. They were infants.

What happened was that I'd decided to teeter the eighty feet across the dam, to explore a densely wooded point, on the other side of which was a secondary pond. I stood with my back to the water, admiring something or other, and heard a crack and saw the afterimage of something on the dash. A pair of ginger fawns, it turned out to be, and clearly seen as they dashed back and forth in front of me in a four-part zigzag. The fifth pass was toward me, by me, and beyond me, with a doubling back on

their part that had them stopping dead still less than five feet away. I had pivoted of course to put my back to the woods and to watch them, thinking *surely* they'd seen me and *surely* they knew they oughtn't come close. They froze. We all did.

And so twin fawns stood before me, only two-and-a-half feet tall and on legs that looked like fingers. Trying to catch their breath, they gasped audibly in and out, their sides pumping quickly and bellowslike over bony ribs. They bleated, sounding like baby goats.

They caught their breath, and in the silence I heard two sounds, or, rather, I heard the absence of sound, twice. It was the noise that is made only by the ceasing of noise. It was the sound of something stopping making a sound. Eerie.

Trying to figure out whether the fawns had their eyes on something behind me or on me, my own eyes flew from one to the other. But there are no visible whites to the eyes of deer, and there is no visible shifting, or at least none that I saw. Then one—oh, Lord—took three steps closer. I wanted to scream: "Be afraid of me, you little dope!" It wanted to sniff. Again there was that ceasing of noise.

And prudence won out. I didn't know what would happen, but I didn't want to be impaled on the sharp hooves of a doe, and I certainly didn't want to get it from behind. So I turned my head. The sniffing fawn froze. I nearly passed out.

Just ten feet behind me stood what I knew was no hallucination. And I knew that my panic was seeing it for me larger than life, but I saw, I was sure, a giant. I seemed to be looking up the legs to the broadest, strongest chest, and beyond that up and up to the hugest ears. The doe looked silver, *was* silver, or else the lights in my brain were about to pop out. Silver hair ringed the ears that were large as radar screens, and the chest was like a shield. Ten feet behind me. I froze, but it felt like melting.

The doe expelled the exhaust from a snort that was so angry it sent the fawns flying. It snorted again and stamped the ground as if to shake the foundations out from under me. Then it fled. Then turned and stamped and snorted, then leapt off again.

As did I, believe me.

I ran like hell until I was sure I was no longer intruding. The doe continued to snort, so I ran back across the beaver dam as if I'd walked tightropes all my life. The adrenaline rush subsided after I sat in a heap on the opposite bank for twenty minutes, getting limp and then limper, and getting back the breath that had flown out like an escapee.

Does and their fawns remain as a family usually for the first two years, the male never being knowingly present. Protection for the fawn comes with its having no scent for the first few days, though it must and can react to noise within minutes of its birth. It has no bacteria in its first stomach, the rumen, and must therefore lick the mother's mouth and eat from the same leaves and nurse for the early months, in order to gain the microorganisms needed for the breakdown of cellulose into sugars that can be absorbed. Doe's milk is exceptionally rich in protein, fat, and solids, three times higher in content than is the milk of a Jersey cow. The fawn quickly matures.

And still it's a gamble. The game turns on a fluke, a chance encounter in the woods one day, an accident. It occurred to me when the fawns stood fifty inches off that I could have snapped their legs like twigs or wrung their necks like washcloths. They were in the gravest danger and were ignorant of it.

What a risky business spring is. A wood-duck mother takes its brood cruising, and seven miniaturizations paddle after in file. A pickerel grabs one of them by the feet and jerks it under, and then there are six. A den is burglarized, nests are robbed, and jellied globs of eggs are gobbled routinely. It is staggering to think that spring has any survivors, given that it is the feast after winter's relative scarcity. A parent nurtures, and then what? Hopes for the best, I guess.

Spring is a table presided over by a stone-faced croupier, raking in the chips with passive disinterest. The house will win in the final accounting. One knows this and bets in order to play. And risks and loses nothing, or everything.

And suddenly the pond is full of the white water-lilies that cover every part of the pond's surface, except the channel the stream still runs through. Their big round leathery leaves almost overlap and are punctuated, like dots for *i*'s and under exclamation marks, by the waxy flowers with pointy white petals. The blooms begin to open going on seven in the morning, when the orange sun begins to burn the white-misted sky to a clearer blue. The tight bud expands to cylinder, then cone, and then it fans wide open to lie on the water surface and repeat itself in its reflection, exposing the yellow starlike hub for most of a day before pulling back from ball to cone to cylinder and again to bud.

The leaves have their breathing pores on their upper surfaces, instead of the more routine underside on land plants, in order that these stomata make direct contact with the air for the exchange of carbon dioxide and oxygen. The root of the plant is food for beavers, and insect eggs have been laid in its stems and on the underside of its leaves. The bullfrog will bask on the rubbery rafts the leaves are, all summer.

The seeds of pond plants are dispersed in various ways, some by the wind that catches the "sail" attached to the seed, and some by the migrators who will transport those that stick to their feet and feathers. Animals often either void or regurgitate seeds they have ingested. Worms, for instance, eat seeds and are eaten by birds who digest the worm and void the seed. Owls and bats regurgitate. Or, cacheing animals will have buried seeds the previous fall and forgotten their location, giving them a chance to germinate.

Likewise, pollination occurs as a by-product. Birds and insects after nectar inadvertently fertilize the flowering plants they flit among. The monarch butterfly pollinates the milkweed it feasts on, the milkweed that is its highly specialized habitat. Only beetles tend to be inefficient pollinators. Rather than move around, they sit and gorge in one place, facilitating nothing but the ceasing of their hunger.

Birds are thought to be attracted not by the scent of nectar but by the color of the flower. Bird-pollinated flowers tend to have guide marks and are vibrant reds or yellows that are harsh and pure. The watery nectar is often the main source of liquid intake for many birds. In summer, birds pant, or cool themselves using their multiple thin-walled air sacs as evaporative surfaces, compensating for their having no sweat glands. The ventilation of the lungs is accomplished in flight, as each downstroke of the wings compresses the sternum and forces exhalation. When birds perch, the bent leg tightens the tendon that runs to the toes, and the bird is thus automatically fixed to its perch and can rest without falling. Feather coloration depends, for blacks and browns, on melanins that are synthesized by the bird, and for reds, oranges, and yellows, on the carotenoids that are taken in with food. Structural color, for example blue, comes with the reflection of blue and the absorption of all other light, and white is due to the reflection of almost all light.

The pond is inhabited by all sorts of birds, many of which have repeated nestings that start in spring and extend well into the summer. Song sparrows may hatch four broods, laying the eggs of the subsequent brood as soon as the previous young can fly. They nest on moist land near the water and are reportedly lovers of bathing as much as singing.

Yellow-bellied sapsuckers nest in live trees in holes drilled up to eighteen inches deep. Their eggs average six and are glossy white. Also glossy white are the five to fourteen eggs of the kingfisher, which hatch into naked young who are born in a nest dug out of the banks of the pond. The female brown-headed cowbird lays many eggs, one per nest, in the nests of others, especially warblers, sparrows, and vireos. If the landlord birds don't either throw the cowbird egg out or rebuild the nest on top of it, its chances for survival are good, since it tends to be bigger than other bird eggs and thus gets more heat from the incubating mother bird. When it hatches, the young cowbird uses its size and relative maturity for snatching food away from the others that often die or are thrown out.

The pied-billed grebe are migrators who spend the summer around the pond, building nests in masses of floating vegetation anchored to live pond weed. Young grebe swim and dive as soon as they hatch and are often swum around by the female, who stows the young under its wings. If alarmed, the mother grebe will dive and swim to the edge of the pond, where it hides in the vegetation, showing only its eyes and its bill. Any young that might have been under the wing are released with the underwater movement of the wing, and they bob to the surface for better or worse.

And the bullfrog all this time has been making its gradual transformation from tadpole, the larval form in which it spends two or three winters, growing to five or six inches before the tiny back legs begin to appear at the base of the tail. First the back legs, then one of the front, and then the other struggles out to correct the off-balance distribution of weight that had the tadpole swimming on tilts and landing on the bottom with bumps. The tail will be resorbed, but gradually, during which time the tadpole is unable to eat. The lungs are being formed to take over from the gills. Then suddenly there are changes in the head. The little oval fish mouth is extended horizontally, and the eyes grow bigger and move up toward the top of the head. The bulb shape becomes contoured as the head takes on its frogginess, and the tail is all but assimilated, which means that by late August the frog is ready to move on to its carnivorous adult diet of insects, snakes, fish, and smaller frogs.

The bullfrog is a solitary and never sings in chorus, even though the bullfrog din sounds like chorusing. It sheds its skin every other day, in one piece, and changes color according to the weather. Water is absorbed through the skin, eliminating the need to drink, and in addition to lungs, the bullfrog has a highly vascularized mouth and pharynx, allowing it to take in air and water directly. The average jump is twenty-six inches for this largest of pond frogs, but its bearing is severely contradicted by the silly *eek!* sound it emits if jumping from fright.

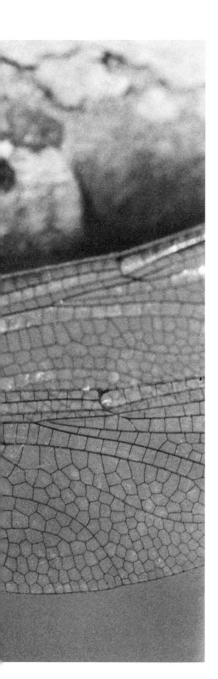

At night in summer the pond makes a foreign-sounding music with its frogs, an atonal drone that persists from dusk until nearly dawn. Sometimes it sounds like a string section tuning up, sometimes like off-key horns, sometimes like madness, a crazy cacophonous discord that strains the nerves, believe me. Sometimes I'm the one I think will shed its skin, in one piece. If I knew how.

But by day the frogs are baskers, and the frenzy belongs to the dragonfly, who swoops to capture its midflight meals of mosquitoes and other insect succulents. Other names, and evocative ones, for the dragonfly are mosquito hawk, snake doctor, water maiden, and devil's darning needle, but the best in my opinion is dragonfly, after the flexible cylindrical body topped with its outsized, powerful head. And after the fact that, like dragons, the dragonfly is awesome.

After the metamorphosis, when the wings have been pumped full of body fluid and dried to a sort of cellophane, the dragonfly can travel at speeds of up to twenty miles an hour. Its wingbeats per second are only twenty to thirty—as opposed to mosquitoes at up to six hundred, and midges at up to a thousand—but no insect can fly as efficiently as the dragonfly with its perfectly synchronized, splendid double set of wings.

And their colors are wonderful: blue dragonflies seem plated with turquoise stones, and black with onyx. The species that is red, and which outlasts the others that die at summer's end, looks like a wooden matchstick struck and flaming. No dragonfly can fold its wings to make itself less conspicuous, but on a warm day it can adjust them to shade the abdomen. Hot days, the dragonfly has to raise its abdomen to an almost vertical relationship with the hot surface the insect rests on.

The water surface on a summer day is marked by the box steps of water striders, who use only four legs for locomotion, the other two being used for picking up food from the water and holding it above themselves to drain before eating. To groom, the water striders tip back on their hind legs and clean themselves with the forelegs, then tip forward and use the hind

to groom. Their water-repellent legs have snowshoe hairs to keep them from breaking through the water surface, and thus they stride.

From underneath, the surface film is shattered by bass which jump after mayflies. The mayfly reaches its sub-imago form in a very rapid transformation from a nymph in casing to winged adult, the speed explainable perhaps because the mayfly is so preyed on at this point in its development that time is literally of the essence. It is the only insect to molt after attaining its adult form, going from sub-imago to imago. The adult mayfly mates and dies without ever eating.

The water flea reproduces itself parthenogenically once the females have hatched, at the time of the ice breakup, from overwintering resting eggs. In spring and early summer the female sheds its carapace containing the brood pouch into the water, and every young is a female water flea, generations of females following every ten days or so. As cold weather comes on, some of these females lay eggs that develop into males, and after mating has taken place the females produce one or two larger, yolkier, stronger-shelled, fertilized eggs, the resting eggs that will hatch into the following year's first generation.

Rare to see but some years found, especially at the end of summer, is the pond jellyfish, the only freshwater jellyfish found in all of North America. In continual motion, circular and revolving, the dime-sized jellyfish rises, pulsating, to the surface, then flips over and drifts down toward the bottom, paralyzing the planktonic animals brushed by its tentacles, and collecting them. Nearing the pond bottom, it turns right side up again and swims to the surface to flip and glide downward, over and over.

But summer isn't only continual motion, isn't only eggs and sap and seeds and pollen, isn't only abundance. Summer is also shortage. An image for this is the tubifex worm, which lives head down in the pond bottom, waving its hind end to create water currents from which to draw oxygen through its body wall. As the oxygen concentration decreases, the tubifex

protrudes farther out to expose a larger body area. Oxygen becomes short in summer, and hard to come by.

Which means that in full summer there is often nothing happening for hours on either side of noon. Turtles, frogs, and snakes will sunbathe on grass tussocks, logs, and rocks, but other coldbloods seek the shade of the pond's vegetation and wait for the heat to go down with the sun. As the water warms, its capacity for holding dissolved oxygen decreases, and the pond's aquatic life has trouble breathing. Since the water is shallow, six feet at most, and since there's a temperature variation of only ten degrees, at most, there are no cool depths to escape to. The water level is low and seems to be shrinking back from its banks, evaporating almost visibly, exposing lush green marsh-grass fringe.

The channel is still clear but is the only part of the pond not clotted with new and old vegetation, growing or decomposing. The edges of the pond are jellied with globs of algae that look like slabs of peanut brittle—the air bubbles trapped in the slime—but have the texture of a seaweed jam. They float, no doubt a function of the same trapped air, and receive the eggs of countless insects, but they clog the surface and inhibit breathing.

Decay bacteria are abundant in proportion to the water's warmth, and therefore in midsummer almost every speck that interrupts the stream of light is a minute organism or an organic particle of decaying plant tissue. One steps on the pond bottom and a trail of bubbles, methane gas from decomposition, rises up to burst on the surface. The shortage in summer is the result of overabundance.

But then as the long afternoon light slants and seems to be finite after all, activity resumes. The cooler water again holds sufficient quantities of oxygen to support the demands of pond life, and there is a sort of general evening resurrection, a second chance. Birds buzz the pond again for insects, beavers cruise, turtles flop back into the water, frogs begin to call, fish jump through the surface and leave behind concentric rings that

133　Summer

ripple off, and a water snake darts its sinewy body in and out of parentheses, swimming.

The sun is a redder orange in setting than when it comes up. Persimmon-colored, it drops, each notch its own diameter, dropping a notch each minute and finally, in a minute, disappearing.

The tint is a cloudy reddish and the water reflects it up to the sky. The drowned-stump snags take on a faint purple and, jutting up through the water, look, though still like thumbs, like bruised ones. Kingfishers perch on them, and tree swallows slip into nests in their hollow interiors. In this faint light one can't see but knows that in a ring around the trunk are the abandoned casings of various insects that stopped off to shed their external skeletons, then flew off on brand-new wings. One knows it because the air is cluttered with flying insects.

A deer comes down to the water's edge and walks in up to the shoulders. At first it drinks and then submerges its head so that only the ears are showing. They twitch and twist as if to scoop up sound while the deer does its underwater grazing. The deer raises its head, its mouth full of vegetation, and chews but also surveys, assessing the danger it is or isn't in. Then it dunks its face under again.

Its eyes glimmer dimly, like topaz, when it comes up again and rotates its head. They glimmer by catching the last of the frail light, reflecting it. At night if you turn a strong light on deer, those eyes don't glimmer, they shine. They shine like headlights.

The crepuscular beaver emerges from the lodge and swims in slow broad arcs the several-hundred-yard distance between the lodge and the dam. It inventories the dam and either does or doesn't make a repair by adding a clump of mud or a branch. The living is mostly easy in summer, and the minimal tree cutting mainly concerned with the acquisition of bark and branches for food. All night, however, one hears the intermittent tail slap that signals the lurking presence of

intruders, and one must be reminded that what goes on at the pond at night goes mostly unwitnessed.

One night I mistakenly rolled out my sleeping bag across a deer trail. I'd picked the spot, but in the dark, because it was roughly where I wanted to be for the dawn. Instead of counting sheep I'd counted the whining buzzes of bullfrogs, but I'd at last, apparently, succeeded. Or succumbed. The next I knew was the snort sound for which I had just one association. Had I, even sleeping, come between doe and offspring? I waved the lit flashlight around like a wand and caught those rhinestone night eyes with it. The deer turned tail and ran. I lay awake for hours.

And what, I thought, am I doing here, where owls are hooting and beavers slapping out alarms, where vexing female mosquitoes siphon my blood, and where I seem to be jeered by the maddening dissonance of frogsong? I was a stranger, and didn't I know that? And not one of night's mysteries was going to come clear for me.

I didn't move the sleeping bag. Instead I lay on my back and looked through the telescope the treetops made, and examined the sky for falling stars. And found them. And found another mystery.

Storm

Another night went even more slowly, long on vampiric insects and the strumming of bullfrogs, short on breezes. The air wasn't slick, as it is when cooled, but syrupy and bulky with heat, and tacky. The night was a burden, but implied was a promise, and I was up with the thinnest light, already watching for the storm.

The hot air from the land was going to collide with the cold in the cumulonimbus clouds that gather up to thirteen miles off the ground, and in which the air is frozen into ice crystals. Called a cell because it is the active center of the storm, the thunderhead and the currents of cold and hot air that make up the cell promise much in the way of both chaos and relief. There will be friction between the negative and positive charges on the ice particles: there will be lightning, and there will be rain.

Bugs I can't identify are ringed with circular ripples, like halos around each contact made with the water's surface. They look, already, like raindrops on water, and so the pond in this first light appears to anticipate what can't come until the heat has intensified almost unendurably, later on. In the meantime let the bugs look like rain.

A beaver leaves the barest wake and makes no noise patrolling the dam, then adds, in three slow-motion efforts, two freshly snipped, leaf-stripped branches and a log hefted up from the bottom of the pond. The log is pressed against the chest by forepaws and fastened by the chin, then heaved onto the dam and kept from rolling by clamps of teeth. The beaver's final pass at maintenance puts a twig on the dam as if a feather in a cap, after which the beaver goes off to go under and into the lodge. The first light is the last it sees until late afternoon.

The water-lily begins to fan open but takes long hours, and the heat seems to accelerate with each increment. By midmorning the lilies are floating in the tepid water, their innards exposed to the broiling sun. I decide to climb the cliff from which there is and overview, and do, but only get there to find that the lilies,

which every other day have stayed open all day long, have this day shut down already and closed back up, as if not to spend all their elasticity meeting the fierce demands of one terrible noon.

I loop my legs over a tree felled and de-barked by beavers in order to rest my feet like lily pads on the water's surface. Of course I hope to cool my heels, but it works not well at all. The water in the haze of this hottest day has the look and feel of bouillon, and it warms me as if I were drinking it on a winter day. It occurs to me that as winter can be deep and dark and bitter with cold, as well can summer be with heat. Bitter-hot is the feeling that every cell has been injected with mildly paralytic toxins, when it feels as if acid runs in the place of blood. On a midday dark in summer the only certain thing is that when it finally rains it will pour. And yet, it isn't yet time.

I push off in the belly boat in hopes of manufacturing a breeze, and to see what else stirs. At the main lodge, the bilge pump that is the raft's ingenious motor, and which makes no more noise than an electric toothbrush, is enough as usual to bring a beaver out from the lodge for a halfhearted slap of the tail that says *"Not you again."* As usual I take that slap for a compliment and keep going.

Some dragonflies will alight every time a cloud obscures the sun, and it seems in this dark and bright afternoon light that the dragonflies are crazy with indecision. I watch a mating pair fix themselves together, and I marvel at the astonishing intricacy of a system in which the genitals of insects are so specialized that dragonflies of different species don't fit, can't interlock, won't mate. The female injects the fertilized eggs into a gelatinous algae mass, and the two blue dragonfly bodies catch a bit of the sun and shine and look like pieces of turquoise crafted into a brooch. The veined bright blue of polished semipreciousness.

Thunder begins to moan over the next county and induces me to quicken my observations. I have paddled the belly boat into a cove and tag a spider that clambers along the grassy bank, by

grabbing one of its very long legs. It has a tiny orange body, on the top and front of which are eight dots I can only see by magnification. Eight eyes, that means, but still the spider is nearsighted, a predator who sits and waits for prey to get snagged. All the simple eyes of a spider can't equal one eye of a dragonfly, which has in each of two compound eyes twenty-five thousand ommatidia, each of which is composed of a hexagonal lens that focuses light on a cluster of sensory cells that record a part of the mosaic image. These wraparound eyes, though immobile, see in all directions all at once; there are three simple eyes—ocelli—that are believed to detect the difference between light and dark. The spider bites me. I let its leg go.

I'm afraid of snakes and would discuss it irrationally and at length if it weren't for the storm coming up. As it is, I see a shed skin and pull it into the boat before, as they say, thinking. It has the look of a sleeve pushed up on an arm, with the part that covered the head folded back to make a deep cuff. I stretch it out to about two feet and touch the fingernail-like circles that would have covered the lidless eyes. It alarms me that it should be so intact, then that I should have found it. Then that I would treasure it.

But I treasure almost everything, as if the pond were a giant junk shop and I its loving proprietor, who overprices everything so it won't be sold. For instance, a pair of dragonfly wings are artfully displayed on a grass tussock. In fact, since the wings are leftovers from the recent meal of what was probably a frog or water snake, they are not displayed at all, they are discarded as inedible. You could have fooled me.

The dragonfly wing is a most remarkable, elegant creation and, in my opinion, one of the most beautiful of all the pond's intricacies. Its fabric is a cellophanelike transparency veined to indicate what species of dragonfly it is or isn't. The two pairs combine to allow for a unique flight mechanism: beating alternately, the beats are timed such that the rising hind wings encounter air that is not made turbulent by the downward-

beating front pair. Such an efficient system in which the wings may vibrate sixteen hundred beats per minute makes the dragonfly capable of flying at its speed of twenty miles per hour; not surprisingly, the muscles that operate these wings weigh a quarter of the total body weight. What I wouldn't give to see what was probably the greatest insect-wing expanse ever to exist, in the dragonfly Meganeura, whose wingspan, but millions of years ago, was three feet across.

In the Carboniferous age insects tended to be the size that birds are today. Fifty million years before there were flying birds and reptiles, there were insects flying on wings that, of all the animal wings, were the only ones not developed as modified legs but instead as specialized structures. Then, as now, insects didn't have lungs and thus took air into their tracheal systems. Was the air three hundred million years ago richer in oxygen? I would guess yes.

I examine my found wings under a glass that magnifies fifteen times. A leaded window is what I see, but a pattern so fantastic that no artisan would have bothered to try for such intricacy, not even taking a lifetime and with the promise that the window would outlive the world. The wonder is that the dragonfly wears wings like that for a lifetime that lasts, at best, a summer.

I focus on the drop of water caught on the wing and look through the drop to see the trees along the far side of the pond, upside down. Through the glass I can see those same trees through the wing, but right side up. The water works as a lens, reversing the image of pointy pines in the circle of space it occupies on the dragonfly wing. It is one of life's simpler discoveries. Or is it? Is mystification ever simple?

We know so little. Only in 1907 was it discovered that eels, as was believed for centuries, don't regenerate spontaneously from mud. Instead these fish spawn in four set breeding grounds around the world, in the North and South Pacific oceans, in the Indian, in the Atlantic. All the eels in North America and Europe hatch in the Sargasso Sea, an area in the Atlantic Ocean south of Bermuda, in the floating jungle mass of the alga *Sargassum,* at two hundred fathoms. The tiny larval thinhead, which resembles a transparent willow leaf, migrates to the coast its species dictates, taking three years if European and one if American. At the coast the males stay behind in salt water, but the females, who have also developed out of the larval form into dark and tubular three-inch elvers, will go inland to fresh, traveling up rivers and streams or underground through channels in the earth to get to the freshwater environment in which they will mature.

Just as you will never find an American eel in Europe, or vice versa, it is believed you will not find a male in fresh water. You will find only a female and only one that has not mated, and any exception is not a true eel. Because what the five- or six-year-old adult female does is to go back to the coast, sensing out particles of salt water in thousands of gallons of fresh and

following them, making its way back to the Sargasso Sea, where it lays ten to fifteen million eggs the re-joining male will fertilize. Then they both die. And 20 percent of all eels in all ponds descend annually to reach the sea, turning silver and fasting for the migration (because the gut has degenerated), and slithering out of landlocked ponds to rivers and on to the ocean, each brimming with millions of eggs. I can barely absorb the news.

How could a creature so unadmired that only certain other cultures can manage to render it a delicacy have, in fact, a way of life that is both routine and heroic? I told a friend about the eels and showed him the dragonfly wing and the water drop under magnification. He said, "You know what the payoff is? There is no science. Only God."

It still hasn't burst. The thunderhead has darkened the sky at two o'clock to the yellowish-gray of a massive bruise. The wind is proclaiming imminence, imminence, turning the leaves underside up, whirling them furiously. The colors are all metallic, but they are pewter, bronze, iron, rather than the cheerier copper, brass, silver, gold of a sunlit day. The noise the wind makes is an alarm.

Since the aluminum tent poles unnerve me as possible lightning attractants, I rig a lean-to, using small trees. It flaps already in the practice wind before the real blow, and I have to wonder if I should be here. I've never before seen the pond so completely evacuated. Everything with enough brains to head for cover has, and I am the lone, exposed observer. The sky is charcoal, and thunder slaps so fiercely that it seems I'm in a concert hall for a matinee performance of the *1812,* or of anything composed by a Russian.

The first rain comes in on an angle, hits the pond's surface, and sends up a tail. It's as if it's checking off, millimeter by millimeter, what it then will rain down upon in deadlier earnest. The water surface, that membrane which is only one molecule thick but which has a greater tensile strength than steel, is shattered into millidroplet particles, and I doubt that even the hydrogen and oxygen atoms can stay adhered to one another. I wonder what the water measurer does, since it is an insect that lives entirely on the surface, never penetrating, grasping prey it pierces, sucking the insides out, if the smaller insect has had the misfortune of falling onto the surface. In the downpour there's no surface left. I think with a kind of amusement that my first observation of the day had been of insects skating on the surface film and looking like raindrops.

Lightning is something we cannot keep pictures of in our minds. I can know as it strikes that I've seen a stroke that is different from every other one (and sometimes at that moment see how), but every stroke then vanishes as if the sight were too transfigured by my alarm to remember distinctly. The alarm, on the other hand, I can carry forward indefinitely. So: the lightning strikes like blows exploding from a parent who won't

take it anymore, or from a child who won't either. It illuminates the pond in a terribly brilliant flash that manages, by force of its sudden unknown violence, to render the pond a painted prop. It becomes irrelevant that the pond is real, against the more real explosion of light, and for that flash it all may as well be painted on canvas, everything, that is, but the zigzag of fury. I take off from my crouch under a smallish tree and run as if to save my life.

Propelled, I fly. Fleet-footed Achilles has fallen arches compared to me, and I dance along the ground on water-repellent legs that ought to be the envy of the surface-dwelling water measurer I was worried about when it was just raining. The grasses and ferns I run through are startlingly green, and the trunks I zigzag myself around are the black of a grease pencil. Ultimate, it all is, or at least so it seems.

And the rain doesn't stop. It modulates itself to the extent that it goes from hard to very hard to extremely hard, and back, but that's it. What it does do, however, is turn a pine tree into a sparkler, the sight of which stops me in my mad tracks.

Because a sparkler is definitely what it looks like. The water is running so fast down each long needle of each cluster that the tree seems to be only the shadow of its illuminated twin. The tree itself is the thing that isn't; what is, it appears, is instead a sparkly overcoat with a hundred thousand glass sleeves.

155   Storm

I wonder if the water has no weight because it so rapidly displaces itself that in effect it planes along the surfaces of the pine. Less water would cause the clusters to droop, just as less speed would have caused me in my running to trip over roots. An automobile leaves an asphalt road at speeds over fifty-five and planes on the intermediate water, gravity outdone for once. A dancer choreographs a fall and recovery to standing that combines speed with upheld weight and barely acknowledges the floor. This is what, I swear, I was thinking about when the first tree went over behind my back.

Without the cracking of trunk, I didn't know until the thud that what was sounding like a tree going down was what it was. Having once cleared a mile of woods for a road, I'm familiar with the groan, the crack, the splintering and swishing of branches before the thud and its dimmer but immediate echo. But never had I heard the sound of red-pine roots being torn from the ground. Nor could I have guessed that a wind I could cut through, running, was going to press a grown pine, as if arm-wrestling with it, from upright to prone.

Like an ambulance I speed the hundred yards to the scene. The gash on the ground has a diameter as wide as I am tall, and the shallow root system seems to have been peeled back like an enormous scab. A fullgrown tree has been plucked from the woods like an ordinary weed and tossed down for mulch.

It lies like a barefooted corpse, the cross-sectioned roots looking for all the world like creased soles of feet. I climb its length as anyone would an eighty-foot tree that is not perpendicular to the ground, and I am glad, coming upon it as I have before its death, that at least I know its Latin name. *Pinus resinosa.*

And suddenly I am tasting salt. All the petty and important losses in my life reverberate through me in indistinct voices. It doesn't matter that it's only a tree blown down, I'm not thinking of trees. I'm thinking of people, and I am grieving.

The three red pines that are to be blown over all go in the same blunt gust in this first and hardest phase, after which there's a false arrest, a tease of calm that turns the pond world lemony, briefly.

The rain again begins and brings out hundreds of ghostly white moths that seem to take to the rain but are the only things that do. After which there's another pause, longer now, that seems to be a dress rehearsal for the post-storm pageant.

The third rain is mercifully succinct but chilly and, the lightning danger passed, I choose to spend it in the pond, whose water is twenty degrees warmer than the rain is.

Then at last the only rain is excess rolling off each standing tree. It is four hours since that first rain angled in, and I take off all my sodden clothes before knowing if the dry ones in the tent still are, or caring. The birches glisten like bands of neon, the pond is smoky glass. The sparkler pine is encrusted with crystalline full-carat water drops. I am breathing the cleanest air ever.

Whirligig beetles congregate in clumps of up to fifty or sixty and nudge one another like bumper cars in amusement parks. They are black pointy ovals with water-attracting undersides and waterproof backs, and their bifocal eyes are for seeing both above the surface of the water and below it. They breathe air on the surface and carry it, when diving, in bubbles underneath the wing cases and at the tip of the abdomen. The bubble works as a gill, its membrane being the interface through which, after the oxygen in the bubble has been removed, more oxygen can be drawn from the water. Eventually the whirligigs resurface, get new air, and dive again. For detecting prey they have sense organs in the antennae that float on the film and pick up signals from the changes in the ripples reflecting from the waves created by their own whirling. I catch a whirligig beetle and hold it in my hands until its wings dry, when it flies back to its congregation to bump and twirl and glide some more.

The pond becomes a cafeteria after the rain. The dragonfly catches insects in the basket it makes with its six spiny legs. A major food factor is mosquitoes, but it will also eat small moths, butterflies, and horseflies it captures from below, and in half an hour it can easily eat its own weight, and keep eating.

With my glass I examine the gluttonous mosquito walking on my knee, the six legs operating like two tripods: front and rear on one side and middle on the other functioning in unison. I watch the proboscis inserted to siphon my blood, a necessity for nourishing the eggs this female will lay in any environment, including a beer can, that will hold water for at least ten days. The bloated mosquito heaves itself into the air and flies off; I scratch my knee and reassert my preference for the male of this species, which doesn't dine on blood but rather on plant juices.

Their own blood, and that of all insects, is circulated by means of a simple unchambered heart that contracts to pump it to the brain and through the body cavity, receives the blood again into its hollow chamber, and pumps it out once more when the chamber is filled. Some species have auxiliary pumps—the back-swimmer beetle has pumps in its legs—and sometimes the heart will beat backward with no resulting ill noted.

The bodies of insects aren't organized around internal skeletons, are instead enclosed within external skeletons made of a complex carbohydrate called chitin. It is not agreed whether chitin is entirely water-resistant or, but very slowly, dissolved by water. For the insect that frequently sheds its chitinous casing, and for the one that lives only briefly anyhow, it is a point with little point. Chitin keeps in moisture, enabling insects to survive hot climates and, because it is indigestible, is excreted in the waste pellets of insects who eat other insects. Science is gathering these chitin pellets and experimenting with them for use in artificial heart valves.

I'm made downright chilly by the crispness of air on skin that has risen up in bumps against it. I see, but everywhere, hair, as if my body were a topographical map, as if I am a landscape in the farming region of some county where crops don't rotate from tobacco to marigolds to peas, where there is but one crop ever, which is long- or short-form rainbow-variety coarse or babyfine hair.

But I can't, as the saying goes, do a thing with it. Consider Dolomedes, the fisher spider. One of the largest animals on the surface film, its body hair works in three interesting ways: to function as sense organs that respond to touch; to trap air so that the spider, who turns silver with trapped air, can breathe underwater for forty-five minutes; and to distribute the body weight evenly over the film once the spider re-surfaces. I've only seen one of these marvelous batik creatures, and only once. Including its legs it had the circumference of a silver dollar. No wonder they are adequate enough hunters to spin webs not for trapping prey but only as a nursery for their young.

I dress in clothes that are at least drier than anything else at the pond, and I decide that even though I could go on watching insects eating and being eaten for the nearly two hours of light that remain, I'm in need of observing a creature that has a chambered heart.

I climb the eighty feet across the longest dam in this pond system, the one I watched get added to in the early morning, and walk around to the main lodge that houses seven beavers: two mating adults, a pair of kits, and three yearlings. I lie on the lodge and listen through the vent to their grooming noises and to their hissing. The odor of their musk is intensified by the damp and has a waxier, more pungent smell than there normally is around the lodge, which smells more characteristically like the bad imitation colognes that are peddled as having a "manly" personality. Spider webs glisten from the leftover rain and combine to create a lovely lace drape over the entire lodge. Since flies are attracted by animal smells, business in the webs is brisk. I don't seem to disrupt it much when I walk around on the lodge to coax the beavers out.

One by one, and only last the kits, the beavers pop up from the underwater tunnels that lead from the lodge. There are bubbles,

then ripples, then the almost noiseless appearance of the brown square head. I am lucky; all seven eventually make it. They glide, cruising silently, disappearing and reappearing. After apparently determining that I am the interference—and I am a nobody—they switch from purposeful cruising to a more aimless sort. There are no more tail slaps to warn one another and simultaneously startle me into giving up my camouflage (whatever that means for a human being I can't imagine; I feel at all moments utterly obvious at the pond), and there is instead only the most tranquil water ballet of a promenade.

Leafy branches are swum from around a bend and taken under into the lodge as food for the kits. The dives, even when they are dragging the food supply, are graceful out of proportion. There are no back legs or tail that break the surface, there is no arching gasp for air before going under; the head, simply and beautifully, goes under. In water ballet there's a name for this dive, but all I remember is its difficulty.

After a while I decide to see what the branches are being clipped from, and I cross the peninsula the lodge is built on and cut around to another facet of the pond's edge, admiring to distraction the slivery wood chips at the base of a ten-inch oak the beavers have recently felled. Aspen is the beaver's much-preferred food, but the beaver will supplement aspen with most any hard- or softwood growing around the pond, except the most common swamp maple, which the beaver hardly ever touches. A five-inch-diameter willow will be felled in three minutes, a six-inch birch in ten. I have heard that not far from the Temper Brook pond is the stump of a white oak felled by beavers, thirty-seven inches across. I take the path that runs between the oak and the closest point of entry into the water, a slipway worn and swept by tail-dragging, and I stop at the edge to survey the water for branch barges. What I don't see, of course, until I am just eight feet from it is a grooming adult.

Since I can't believe that with all its fine sensory equipment the beaver doesn't know I'm there, I believe it simply chooses not to acknowledge me. In any event, I am allowed to observe the complete grooming routine. It begins at the head, where the

reddish-orange fur is waterproofed by the forepaws with oil collected from the multipurpose orifice at the base of the abdomen. The strokes are between those of a cat washing its face with curled licked paw and those of a human being running both hands back from the face through the hair. Persistent, meticulous, the beaver's grooming has to do with keeping the body from getting wet, thus with keeping it buoyant

With its hind feet, which have the specialized double nail on the second toe of each, the beaver combs the luxuriant brown body fur, cleaning it of leeches and other parasitizing debris. It twists the top half of its body to let the hind foot at those hard-to-get places, and then it oils this bulk, looking like a girdled person smoothing fabric over huge hips. I can't decide if this beaver reminds me of a dowager in black kid gloves to the elbow—with her receding chin and buck teeth, looking silly in a fur coat in August—or of Dostoyevsky's narrator in his *Notes from the Underground,* the slob who's lived in a bathrobe for twenty years.

With beavers there is no way to tell sex (except in season by nursing teats) without going inside the cloaca, the opening leading to the genitals, the urinary ducts, and the rectum into which empty oil from the oil glands and musk from the castor glands. Both sexes grow continuously from birth to death— beavers are the only mammals who do—and there is no size variation to differentiate male from female. Consummately androgynous, the forty-pound beaver before whom I stand transfixed is, I am certain now, both the dowager and the slob.

After what I guess to be ten or twelve minutes, the beaver tips forward onto its forelegs and sweeps the large oval of a rubbery tail around to behind. In two steps it is in the water, pushing off from the shore with hind feet, paddling, the tail its rudder. It floats in lazy curves and, as if to amuse us both, rotates its head from side to side, expelling air through its nostrils to make bubbles. I am charmed.

At last I am at rest. The tension from this long day of isolation that began on sleep-short nerves and scared the daylights out of me during the storm runs down my shaft like an elevator and drains out my feet. I am drained from being both two miles from everywhere and at the center of everything, and from having been abandoned during the storm by every living thing that doesn't photosynthesize. I'll go home now.

I recross the dam and collapse my tent. The toppled pines that lie on their southeast–northwest diagonal look from the root end like tombstones with extremely long shadows. I tighten my laces and load up to hike out for the car. Only four more observations will I make today.

First, fungi. The rain has made them jewels, and seven varieties wink up at me as if from display cases. Tiny scallops, dark brown piped in white; olive green with beige ruffles; seashell shapes striped from gray-blue-green to gray-tan-brown; a cluster of coffee-colored hooded mushrooms that look like china monks; a solitary flaming disk; flattops with the color and texture of pumpkin skin; orange-gold Day-Glo globules that look like resin, or plastic.

A side stream pulsates with water and zippers down the back of a hill and into the beaver pond. Ferns the color of young lime skins have grown in a thatch across the stream bed that's usually dry in summer. The flood has flattened those in the bed to give the tousled thatch a center part.

Tree swallows in iridescent bluish-green sweep across the pond to skim off insects. They seem all pointy wing and tail as they pivot and dip and glimmer.

A swamp maple overhangs the pond and rains the water from its leaves. Each drop as it hits the surface ripples it, ringing itself concentrically. And the day is symmetrical: insects in the first light look like drops of rain, in the last it's the other way around.

Fall

The autumn-morning mist turns cobwebs into crocheted doilies spun from glistening threads. They hang between uprights, suspended like hammocks, and billow like spinnakers, fixed at the corners by guy wires gauged to give a little with the wind. The web's architect and landlord, the spider, is an arachnid, which means it has eight legs, two body parts, and no antennae. In insects, the first pair of legs become antennae or are discarded, so that insects have six legs and three-part bodies. Instead the spider's first pair of legs are modified into chelicerae, fanglike pincers with which the spider subdues the prey that haplessly lands in its net.

The water is black and is faster moving. Bubbles of foam from way upstream tumble over the dams and swirl in the dug-out pools on the downstream side of the dams. The surface of the pools seems to be glass stroked by paintbrushes. I'm not certain why the water is black, except that every color at the pond has deepened and, perhaps more to the point, the water is full of decaying plant tissue.

Desmids are algae with unicellular bodies, bent or straight, that resemble little cigars. They are green and are found in large numbers in spring, and in fall in abundance around decaying plant matter. In the fall the water practically bulges with desmids. And also various species of worms, which live in the muddy bottom and banks and feed on decomposition.

Beavers begin in fall to gather branches for the food cache and limbs for the fortification of the lodges and dams. Tree felling begins in earnest in October, and from the edges of the pond back sometimes a hundred feet there are scattered trunks that look like the sharpened ends of pencils. One tree in five never falls to the ground but catches in the branches of others and hangs there uselessly. For the most part, however, the trees go down quite neatly. The bark is stripped and eaten, and the body of the tree is dragged to the water and swum almost into place, then hefted or wedged according to need.

There are scent mounds along the water's edge, two to seven or more per colony. A mound is made of mud and decayed

vegetation piled up to two feet high and scented liberally with the musk of every member of the colony. Musk is produced in the castor glands that are located under the skin near the back legs, emptying into the rectum. The glands may grow to the size of an orange and together weigh a quarter pound; the castoreum is orange-colored and is thick and pungent. The purpose of the scent mounds is thought to be territorial or, because during breeding season both sexes discharge increased amounts, to signal readiness to breed. R. D. Lawrence believes, but is the only one I've found who does, that beavers build their mounds as grooming or resting stations, and that the increased height is advantageous for seeing, hearing, and smelling. He theorizes in *Paddy* that by virtue of sitting on the mound to groom, the beaver deposits its musk and thus, though as a by-product, marks the bounds of its territory.

Play is almost unknown among rodents, but beavers seem to engage in a lot of play, especially a kind of wrestling that amounts to shoulder-to-shoulder shoving. They also clean each other's face and frequently nuzzle. In fall one sees much of the beaver, since fall is the season of busy readying for the semidormancy of winter and the birthing in spring. The lodges must be made secure and the dams more sturdy. Every fall morning at the pond stands for progress made the previous night, beginning at dusk and lasting to dawn. Progress always means recycled trees.

The water level has gradually decreased, and by late fall it has dropped substantially below the leaves of the arrowhead plants. The pointy leaves are left literally high and dry, and they hang in curled droops from the plant stems like flags from poles.

The ferns have turned yellow and then rusty and look singed at the edges, then burnt entirely. They look, after the frost that kills their leaves, like skeletons, or like the shadows they formerly cast. In contrast is the peppermint that grows in the stream in a shelter of rock, and that is still a vivid green, more than ever against the water's black.

177   Fall

The acorns have been separated from their beret-shaped caps, and the floor of the forest is littered with empties. The nuts have been eaten or stashed away for winter meals. Mushroom caps are missing from their stems, likely eaten by squirrels, who apparently are unaffected by those fungi that are toxic. I'm tempted to gather mushrooms myself, and once did but quit when I picked a tan one with a flaky top like crushed dry cereal. Touching it numbed my fingers, so I left them all for creatures who are more knowledgeable.

I don't know a single mushroom's name and instead simply see them as part of the nubby texture the woods have. Stark albino mushrooms are glossy, and sodden brown matte-finish mushrooms have hides that look untanned. Cartoon mushrooms grow in a clump, each one a seven-inch cylinder of a beige foam rubbery substance with a darker, upholstered cap that has a tiny hole in its center.

Berries are everywhere. One bush has them in colors ranging from aqua to black, the majority being a deep bluish-purple and looking like wonderful wooden beads not strung but clumped, as grapes are. Trillium makes a carpet of paisley-patterned low-growing triplet leaves fastened, it seems, by a delicate white flower in spring and in fall by a shiny bright red single berry. Trillium covers the ground in woods whose soil is boggy and acidic.

The mosses are sumptuous. Spongy underfoot, and velvety, certain varieties are descendants of prehistoric vegetation. A three-inch-high relic that covers our floors was once, a quarter of a billion years ago, tree-sized, and these club mosses can take up to twenty years to complete a life cycle. I get down on my hands and knees to examine another moss that's constructed, as a conifer, of clusters of leafy outgrowths that combine to make star shapes. The seedcase sticks up as on an antenna and looks under magnification like the hairy shell of a coconut. It slips off like a cap to reveal a tiny cylinder at the tip of which are the lime-green powdery spores the wind releases. The cap is a quarter inch long, and the spool inside about an eighth inch. Fall is the season for seed dispersal.

And so it is for cattails, whose brown plush bodies split in autumn and lose their stuffing of woolly white along with the seeds the wind blows all along the contours of the land. The cattails look like toy stuffed animals with broken seams, and they remain in this state for half the year.

The trees are beginning to bald, and as a man does, they lose their leaves through thinning first on the top and then at the sides. The colors have appeared slowly with the gradual withdrawal of sunlight and lowering of temperature, which cause a breakdown in chlorophyll and thus the retreat of greens. With no green to overwhelm the other pigments in the leaf, the "natural" yellows and oranges that are present all year become dominant. In addition, the sugar clogged in the leaf, because it isn't processed by photosynthesis, encourages the formation of a red pigment that turns the leaf, depending on the alkalinity or acidity of the sap, either shades of purple or shades of red. The toasty brown of oak leaves in fall is the result of a fourth pigment, tannin.

This fall the weather has not conspired to set the landscape on fire with reds. Most days have been cloudy, if not rainy, which cuts down on sugar production and also, therefore, on crimson. Most trees have had to make do with the recessive colors, showing off only the ever-present yellow and orange that come in a dimmer and duller second after red. The frost we assume to be an intensifier of color isn't. Instead it inhibits all pigment fabrication.

As always the willow is last to forfeit its green, and the last to lose its yellow leaves. It seems the birch is first to shed, with the orange maple leaves somewhere in the middle on the tenacity scale. The leaves are drying as they turn color, since water is sealed off from them by a belt of cells that sever the connecting plant tissue in the stem. The dehydrated foliage falls, and the billions of leaf scars are healed by the growth of specialized cells. A shed tree in front of a still-colored one seems a double exposure, an external skeleton, seen from across the pond. Up close, the process is seen as what it is: emaciation.

Deer browse in earnest, stripping the lowermost branches of leaves before there is time for them to decline. The trails are well worn, since much traveled, and deer droppings clump on the trails as if they were bowls or small baskets of shiny black bean-shaped berries. The mating for the birth in June takes place in November.

The female crayfish spawns in April, picking its abdomen clean of debris and laying several hundred eggs, which attach to the little fan-shaped swimmerets. By July the hatchlings are an inch long and leave the parents' burrow to start their own. Now in November the juvenile crayfish molt into the adult form and mate. They burrow throughout the winter.

All fall there's a downward migration at the pond. Those animals that live high in trees go lower, those that are high-shrub animals move to low bushes, and those that are ground dwellers retreat to positions under logs or rocks or pond weeds. In the water, the migration is also downward: insect nymphs creep lower down the stems they live on and are joined by surface-dwelling beetles; fish leave the shallows for deeper water or to burrow into the bottom; frogs and turtles hibernate in the mud. Cold-blooded animals can't regulate their body temperatures internally and therefore remain barely active, hibernating on land as do salamanders and snakes, or underwater, as do frogs, who breathe through their highly vascularized skin, and turtles, who breathe by inhaling and exhaling water through the anus. Warm-blooded animals either adjust, or hide, or flee.

Eagles, both golden and bald, flee Maine and Canada for the relatively temperate climate of Massachusetts. Each meets its food needs of half a pound a day by midmorning, and soars or perches the rest of the day. An eagle can spot a hare from a distance of one mile; in flight it can move in on its prey at a speed of two hundred miles an hour. Eagles mate for life and rear four young every five years or so, though no breeding pairs have been observed in Massachusetts.

The great horned owl is a permanent resident of the pond area. It has, as do all night-hunting owls, huge light-collecting eyes whose iris and pupil fill the eye socket. Since these eyes are immobile, the owl will swivel its head in a pivot that goes past 180 degrees to create the weird effect of having eyes in the front of the head, in back. Its ears are asymmetrically placed, which facilitates picking up sound on both the vertical and horizontal planes. Its plumage is soft and loose to deaden its own sound in flight, allowing owls to be silent fliers and powerful predators on smaller animals and, cannibalistically, on each other. In autumn they are most audible, probably because the frogs have piped down. And in autumn they are most appropriate. The eerie hooting embodies fall and, because it echoes in the hollowness, also disembodies it.

Ducks and geese are passing through, dropping down to feed and rest at the pond. They have molted in summer, shedding feathers symmetrically in pairs from the wings and tail to preserve their aerodynamic balance, and as if to postpone the post-molt period of their inability to fly. They take off on new plumage with fall's arrival and wing their way south. The Canada goose has been spotted flying over the Himalayas, where the air at 29,000 feet contains only 30 percent of the oxygen contained in the air at sea level. All migrating waterfowl can fly up to sixty miles per hour, faster than our current laws allow on expressways. Many fly by night and by day.

One evening I went to a marshland near Boston to watch the same ducks and geese I'd seen there in the spring heading north. I knew, because the Temper Brook pond was daily full of migrators, that Great Meadows would be fuller yet. The wetlands refuge contains three thousand acres of the swampy habitat migrators favor, and I was counting on being overwhelmed again by numbers. Stalking mallards and Canadas, I was delighted by their hundreds bobbing through the duckweed-clotted surface after vegetation and showing the white of their undersides with each dunk forward. Hundreds, I counted happily.

I walked the sort of causeway that divides the upper and lower ponds and stood admiring. And then I noticed the oddest thing. I saw through the only hole there was in the clouds a blimp. The clouds were backlit and piped in silver and looked, on their own, surrealistic. The blimp, I thought, must be painted onto the sky by Dali. It poked through the hole in the sky like a silver finger but also like a joke. The Goodyear blimp which the week before overhung the World Series was floating its bloated self right over this wetlands motel. But whatever for?

The speed of sound can't be all that fast, I thought to myself, because it seemed minutes before I heard the racket it made, and by then the air above the farthest edge of the water was shot full of birds. The blimp was coming in a straight line from

bottom to top and would pass directly over my head if I was or
wasn't lucky (I hadn't yet decided which was which). Its sound
was the most unmuffled I have ever heard, and it sailed so
low it could have been the top floor of a building in some
low-profile city.

It seemed to be a mammoth magnet, pulling birds out of the
water beneath it and drawing them up to it. Wait a minute.
The blimp was nowhere near me yet, and yet there were already
hundreds of waterfowl wheeling up. Already hundreds, not
counting a one of the hundreds I'd counted.

Thousands, it turned out, tens of thousands. They spun in the
air like wind-troubled leaves in spirals that dove down and up
and inside out, and no two collided. Like leaves, and then more
like motes of dust in the streak of sunlight that funneled
through to put its setting glow on the landscape and transform
the ungainly blimp with flapping guy wires into a sleek sphere
of flame. Like motes, and still no two collided.

I guess it took twenty minutes, not less, for the blimp to
disappear through another slit in the clouds. And another ten
before what you might call order began to be restored, as the
fowl quit their frantic acrobatics and, in waves, dropped back
onto the water. I counted a minute later, once again, only
hundreds.

I'm told it costs the Goodyear people millions to maintain their
four blimps, and that the average cost per flight hour works out
to something absurd: twenty-four hundred dollars. That puts a
price tag on my twenty minutes of eight hundred bucks, and
the silly thought occurs to me that if Goodyear had come
around afterward to collect its fee for the show it put on for me
for free, I'd have gladly paid.

Other things are perhaps more miraculous, but I wonder sometimes if anything is more astonishing than migration. How birds and animals *know* without their AAA maps and guidebooks, to put it trivially, is a question that is fundamentally answerless. They know, that's all. They have to know for the race to endure. But *butterflies* know? It seems one thing for hawks and caribou to know; they are bulky. But butterflies are wisps, and everyone has seen them buffeted by breezes and turned inside out by winds as if they were umbrellas. But butterflies know.

There are scientists whose lives have been devoted to the migratory habits of the monarch and who conclude, through having discovered overwintering sites in Mexico, that the monarch can fly to and from, logging, as a conservative estimate, twenty-five hundred miles in their one-year lifetime. What is understood is that each summer's last generation of monarch is different physiologically (in that a juvenile hormone checks maturation of the adult sex organs) and behaviorally (in that it doesn't mate). The last generation of summer, urged by decreasing daylight and temperature, flies south and winters in a semi-stupor, then flies north, finally mates, and dies.

I've heard what sounds like a myth about monarchs, but which I can't verify either way, and this is it: monarchs migrating across the Gulf of Mexico make a giant raft of their bodies, the ones on the bottom sacrificing themselves by drowning, to preserve the ones on top. And millions upon millions survive to make it to the resting place; it is guessed that perhaps one hundred million monarchs rest in a Mexican site less than four acres large. My feeling is that were I ever to see a hundred million monarchs, I'd either die on the spot or live forever.

There are photographs in magazines that show entire landscapes encrusted with monarchs: trees that barely have their own outlines, a sky that is orange and brown, not blue. One day in late November several years ago, I was in a state park in northern California, somewhat near Monterey. I was entering a cypress grove by way of a eucalyptus grove and was sucking into my lungs the perfume of eucalyptus and looking down to admire and then pick up and sniff and put in my pocket as many of the button-looking fragrant nuts as were going to fit. And I think I was humming.

I heard a "Pssst!" and a stranger to whom I'll be ever grateful, who sat like a statue on a stump, moved a finger, pointing it silently up. Up I looked and saw I don't know how many monarchs, two thousand perhaps, and like barnacles they were. I squatted in place and shared the spectacle with the stranger, my brain ablaze both with the fact of seeing and of nearly having not seen that the trees were in effect embroidered.

What that grove was, I later learned, was one of the western wintering sites, a modest version of the spectacular finds in Mexico discovered only several years ago by zoologists (though, ironically, discovered who knows how much earlier by the cowherds of the Sierra Madre whose cattle graze all winter on monarchs). The climates are similar: cool but not cold, and humid enough to prevent desiccation.

The energy source for all monarchs is the common milkweed. The eggs are laid on milkweed plants, and the larvae feed on the leaves, conserving this energy throughout metamorphosis and converting it to fat stored in the adult's abdomen. It is believed that this final virgin generation is fueled for its migration by this stored fat that accounts for one-third of the total body weight. Productive ovaries do not generally develop in the female until the end of this wintering period. And though less is known about the northward migration, it is thought that the northbound monarchs, who migrate individually, stop off to lay eggs along the way, and that it is this first spring generation that continues north to breed all summer. It may be that the returnees are several generations removed from the monarchs that migrated south in fall, which, if true, would support what is believed: that monarch migration isn't learned but is instead a complex behavior pattern that is inherited.

The cycle begins with the pinhead-size egg fastened to the underside of a milkweed leaf. After three to twelve days the caterpillar hatches, to gorge on milkweed leaves so that in two weeks' time its body weight has been multiplied twenty-seven hundred times. The last of its five molts during this two-week larval period occurs after the caterpillar, having stopped eating, has woven around itself a dense silk casing. The final shed reveals the pupa known as the chrysalis, the pouch from which the adult emerges approximately two weeks later.

It is a striking relationship between monarch and milkweed. The large cups of nectar attract many insects, and whereas the deep, tight slot between the paired pollen masses will easily trap smaller and weaker insects who will die there, the leg or proboscis of the butterfly slips into the slot and picks up pollen that is brushed on the stigma of the next flower. The milkweed leaves contain carbohydrates, 81 percent of which can be converted into fats by the monarch. Some milkweed contains poisons that are advertised by the monarch's distinctive coloration and slow lazy flight, and that render the monarch inedible by birds. Birds either altogether avoid the monarch and its clever mimic, the viceroy, or learn to ascertain the toxicity level, which is relative to the species of milkweed the monarch larva fed upon.

In the early fall two explosions occur, the first being the emergence of the last generation of monarchs, and the second being the bursting of the milkweed pod. Both are crucial.

As the adult becomes ready to break out of the chrysalis, the color of the pouch will change from a pale green-blue to a blackish-green to an inky black. A fluid seems to release the adult inside the casing, at which point the shell becomes transparent and one can see that inside, like a parachute in a case, are the folded, patterned monarch wings. The chrysalis is entirely elegant at this point and highlighted by the points of gold that ring it and that serve apparently to control the development of color in the wings. What looked like a miniature grenade looks now like nothing comparable; but it is a grenade.

 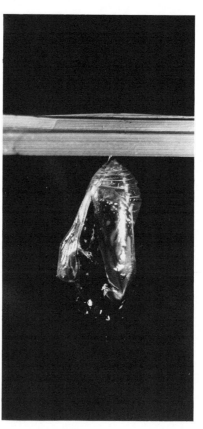 

Since they go off during the night, one has been brought to the lab for photographs. We peer at it expectantly for eight hours, watching it slowly darken, ripening as if it were a grape. We admire its every transformation as if our compliments had the slightest effect of speeding up the process, but we learn instead what we already knew, that nature can't be rushed and that enormous amounts of time are spent waiting for the exactly proper moment for progressive change to take place. We wait and wait more. In the ninth hour, it happens.

There are contractions, and then a portion of the casing, a sort of flap for an envelope, splits open like a trapdoor, and the monarch slides out as down a chute. Its tongue is part of the flap the way a vein is on a leaf, and the tongue will fix the butterfly until the torso is altogether free of the case and it can grasp with its legs, at which point the tongue is reeled in. Then the monarch hangs to dry its fleshy wings and inflate them by pumping fluid through them. It hangs and pulsates for hours before it is ready for flight, but its descent from the chrysalis takes a matter of seconds. Too bad if you miss it, to say the least.

A summer monarch is ready to mate three days after it achieves adulthood, but this is fall. More likely, and more incredible too, is that this one will fly to Mexico. We release it most respectfully.

And I go directly to the pond to look at the others we might have brought back but hadn't. They hang, some pale, some dark, some empty, and I want to call for bugle fanfare. It seems to me impossible, the way miracles go unacknowledged. But unacknowledged it wasn't, and I'll tell you why. A milkweed pod had burst at the top of the stem from which hung an empty chrysalis. Its sides had been rolled back like the door flaps of a tent, and the seeds, which are packed in tight spirals and each attached to a feathery parachute of fluff, were being flown off by the wind. What better way to celebrate the birth of a monarch than with the promise of a new generation of milkweed.

Freeze

Let me contrive a metaphor: a football has been propelled with force along a long low arcing trajectory, and as it travels forward it spins, and as it spins the lacing appears and disappears. The lacing is to the football what winter is to the year. Both are what you notice most as the sphere is being revolved.

And the reason one notices winter most, its demands aside, is that winter is the one time of year when the landscape seems not to resemble itself. The other three seasons are variations on one another: the leaves are either yellow-green, or green, or yellow, depending; in winter there are no leaves. The landscape is not the landscape but the absence of the landscape. Winter is the negative image of the rest of the year.

Once the leaves are gone, winter slips in to put up its decorations piece by piece. The dew point and the freezing point intersect, and morning means hoarfrost's investing membrane of ice crystals formed on all the surfaces, making patterns of a feathery delicacy or grand as plumes. The dry leaves crinkle underfoot, and the moss is crusty. The grass tussocks squeak. Each berry wears a frosty slip and makes the slightest *toc* sound rubbing other berries. Any bush with leaves still on it can be shaken naked, the stiff curled leaves rushing off with a clatter.

The pond gets its first thin skin of ice the first night the cold is bitter enough. This earliest ice is clear and perfect and looks to be an untinted gel that is bonded onto the single-molecule thickness of the water surface. It captures duckweed and other minutiae and holds them fast; I break a jagged slab and, lying on my back at the edge of the pond and holding the ice across my eyes like prescription glasses, pretend to see the sky as if I were one of the aquatic millions. Tiny air bubbles pockmark the undersurface of the ice and cluster and are strung like glass beads no bigger than pinheads. I can see so much in the ice, and especially with my magnifying glass, I dismiss my usual inclination to melt a piece of it in my mouth. I don't want to jam up my system with someone else's overwintering eggs.

The ice will not again be so pretty. A day of warmer weather will temper its clarity and turn it milky; the pond bottom won't then again be visible until spring. But it's not yet strong enough to lie across and be used as a glass-bottomed boat. It has formed first around what it can attach to (stalks, snags, and banks) and from there spread out as if a spill. I am impatient and want it unified, want to be able to walk on it while it is still black and looking like water, and want to peer through it and spy on the creatures for whom the ice is a ceiling. For now, I can only admire the way it makes stiff little skirts around each upright, and the way it gathers itself into masses that freely float about the surface as if they were the reflections of clouds passing overhead.

Thoreau wrote about the character of ice the way he wrote about people, a spare inventory of strengths and weaknesses. He says in *Walden:* "Ice is an interesting subject for contemplation. They told me that they had some in the ice-houses at Fresh Pond five years old which was as good as ever. Why is it that a bucket of water soon becomes putrid, but frozen remains sweet forever? It is commonly said that this is the difference between the affections and the intellect."

Brittle intellect is what ice is, especially compared with a patch of plankton of the same dimensions, which is an undulating syrupy stew, an oozing, groping sensualist whose affections bloom and spoil in a season. Ice is crisp as a cracker, precise as a ballerina, neat and disciplined. But bound. Water travels the earth and ice barely budges; in this way water is complex and ice is simple. So water and ice, like the affections and the intellect, have their assets and have their faults.

The Canada geese who are late on the migration trail group together at the pond's center and rest, if that's the right word, by standing on one leg on the ice and tucking the head and bill under a wing. Or they float in the channel the stream will be until, last to surrender, the ice seals it over. And one by one or few by few they take off and go for an abbreviated spin, then come down to resettle, not unlike myself, whom the chill moves every now and then to fly out of my crouch, spin around, settle back. It is early December and, if you ask me, no time to hang around endlessly. In fact, if I had a home down south I'd have been long gone.

A beaver exits from the lodge underwater and, in surfacing, butts through a thin clear shelf of ice. It is not inadvertent: the beaver means to keep the water open as long as possible. Its tail is used to shatter the surface, to keep access easy, and to prolong the tree-cutting season. Once the pond is shut in, the beaver is not seen again for months. This one swims along the stream path down to the dam. The ice clings to the dam like a fringe the beaver sweeps to a side in climbing partway out of the water and looking, or so it looked to me, over the top and down into the lower pond as if surveying. It doesn't add to the dam, only turns and pushes off to swim back upstream and go under, presumably into the lodge. This in-between season is like that, a preoccupation with trying to keep options open.

Jastrow and, separately, Sagan are scientists who have lately published schemes which, as a way of making available to the public a basic understanding of evolution, describe evolutionary history as a year in which, on the last day of the year and in its last few hours, humans appear for the first time. This strikes me as a good way of dramatizing what relative newcomers we are: even the apes from which we descend appear only after lunch on December 31.

What this has to do with the beaver keeping its options open is that the process of evolution is exactly that. The earth evolves and every species adapts, and sometimes considerably, in order to exist. And we are the new kids on the block. I always feel this at the pond, that the pond revolves like a ball in the air, and I am not born yet. What spring and winter mean for me are only the airiest abstractions of what they mean at the pond. I am not twice a year directly involved in ensuring the continued life of my species; when winter comes I merely turn the heat up, in spring I open windows. You see? What I do is not unrelated to what goes on at the pond, but it is abstracted.

Evolution is divided, like a year into seasons, into eras. Human prototypes evolved late in the Tertiary period and succeeded into the Quaternary as *Homo sapiens* about a million years before Christ. The pond sometimes seems to be a time capsule dating from that earlier period. The multiplication of the one-cells in spring and the downward migration in winter have a once-and-for-all feverish quality. Human beings are irrelevant because, one gets the feeling, we are not yet present. The pond is ancient and foreign and unknowable. And we with our furnaces and windows will never experience what it was like before the frontal lobes in the brains of primates evolved, before man stood and balanced with the help of two big toes and looked down on it all.

I have watched the pond go about its business and only now, nearly at the year's end, does it strike me with force that I haven't been participating. The pond is ancient and I am only an embryo.

It snows for the first time. There has been the pelletized ice of frozen rain, but not yet the crystallized water vapor snow is. The pond is utterly silent. Water vapor is condensing on the nuclei of snow and forming tiny ice needles on which condensation builds up to make a snow crystal. Every crystal is formed on a variation of six, and yet no two snow crystals are identical. Simple crystals come from high altitudes, where there is less water vapor, and lower altitudes produce crystals that can be unspeakably intricate. Snow forms and falls and lands and never makes a sound.

I stand in the open, on the pond's ice, and invite the snowflakes to land on me, each snowflake being a random collection of fabulous crystals. I am a millionaire, I say, and conceive for the first time with any success of what an *oyamel* tree in that clearing in Mexico experiences when its every surface is hidden by massing individual butterflies. I'm rich, I shout.

It falls with an inimitable grace and lands, because newly fallen snow contains a lot of air, the way a whisper lands. It is good for the ground to have this airy snow for a cover: snow insulates with two times the efficiency of sand, and as an insulator it works to reduce heat loss from the lower ground and to keep the soil temperature nearly constant. But I can't wait for it to cover. The sky is gray, as if the day's last light has gone into making snow white, and I've only enough time to pick my way along the narrow dirt roads that used to belong to Mill Village.

The stone walls are frosted raisin breads, and the evergreens are dusted with confectioner's sugar. The pond has altogether the look of one of those glass ball paperweights that, given a shake, make a snowy landscape that's not just snowy but *full* of snow, jam-packed with it. The pond couldn't contain more snowflakes unless each was smaller.

I'd truly love to stay the night and listen to the stillness and watch it. For once I wish the village were still inhabited, with a kitchen belonging to someone who would welcome me in. I'm the only one still out this dim late afternoon, and the only witness I know of to this boundless beauty that wants to be

shared but then again doesn't. The reason I'm the only one here is that I don't belong here at all. The ones who belong have gone underground or gone fleeing to winterless climates. The show—this winter invitational—is a gratuity.

What it means specifically is the end of my year. The pond goes on endlessly repeating itself and will deepen into the fullness of winter and then decline, and then burst into spring and enrich itself with summer and fall, and then again submit. The first ice and the first snow are the acts of submission, and they are also signals to me that I, who would have to repeat myself were I to stay, am on my way. It's the fundamental difference between the observer and what's being observed.

I have already seen each season entirely full of itself and leave with the coming. It has been mine in a funny way, this place in which I don't belong. I give it back.

A Note About the Author

Alexandra Marshall was born in 1944 and grew up in a suburb of New York City. She graduated with degrees in French from Wheaton College and Columbia University. She is married to the author James Carroll, and they live in Boston. In 1977 Ms. Marshall published the novel *Gus in Bronze.*

2